Babbie Mason is a special gift from the Lord. Her life has been filled with wonderful experiences and lessons from God that have helped create songs and lyrics that bless people everywhere. Babbie is not just a talented gospel singer, but also a writer and communicator of the Word who uniquely connects with the minds and hearts of her listeners.

Babbie's own life has had its share of problems and pain, so she writes powerfully yet sympathetically. In *Treasures of Heaven in the Stuff of Earth*, you will feed on the eternal truths that can transform the difficult challenges we all face into beautiful new expressions of God's love and grace.

—Pastor Jim Cymbala
The Brooklyn Tabernacle

Treasures
OF
HEAVEN
IN THE STUFF OF
EARTH

BABBIE MASON

CREATION
HOUSE

TREASURES OF HEAVEN IN THE STUFF OF EARTH by Babbie Mason
Published by Creation House
A part of Strang Communications Company
600 Rinehart Road
Lake Mary, Florida 32746
www.creationhouse.com

Unless otherwise noted, all Scripture quotations are from New King James Version of the Bible. Copyright © 1979, 1980, 1982 by Thomas Nelson, Inc., publishers. Used by permission.

Scripture quotations marked AMP are from the Amplified Bible. Old Testament copyright © 1965, 1987 by the Zondervan Corporation. The Amplified New Testament copyright © 1954, 1958, 1987 by the Lockman Foundation. Used by permission.

Scripture quotations marked NIV are from the Holy Bible, New International Version. Copyright © 1973, 1978, 1984, International Bible Society. Used by permission.

Incidents and persons portrayed in this book are based on fact. Some names and details, however, have been changed to protect the privacy of individuals.

Library of Congress Catalog Card Number: 00-102929
International Standard Book Company: 0-88419-725-5

0 1 2 3 4 5 6 7 VERSA 8 7 6 5 4 3 2 1
Printed in the United States of America

To my loving mother, Georgie Wade,
and the precious memory of my father,
Reverend Willie G. Wade (1922–1987).
A daughter couldn't ask for finer parents.

You taught me how to love God and people,

To love the church, from the steps to the steeple.

Your example, your counsel, your marriage, your ministry

Are trophies of God's grace, a heritage, a legacy.

I've been taking notes on your life, the pains and pleasures;

You've strengthened me through my own stuff to find
hidden treasures.

And what treasures they are, the old and the new;

I owe all that I am to God and to you.

Acknowledgments

For the past decade and a half I have had the blessed privilege to be a songwriter. Like a prayerful and doting mother, I have often called the songs God gives me "my babies." The ideas are conceived, and they begin to take shape. Sometimes through inspiration, sometimes through perspiration, each song is brought into the world. Some stay close to home. Others leave home and go to the uttermost parts of the earth to impact the lives of others. I hear and read about them. Sometimes it's like a sweet reunion when I hear them sung by others. They come back home to my heart, all grown up, having endured the tests of time. Each song is unique and special.

The family is expanding. I am honored to welcome this book, a brand-new member, into the world. I know that babies don't come into the world by themselves. It takes a number of gifted people who work together as a unit to make it all happen. In the same way, it took a lot of very gifted and dedicated people to take this book from a seed of a dream to a colorful reality. So, I want to say thank you to the following people for the part they played:

To my loving, patient and faithful husband, Charles: You have encouraged me in every way. To our sons Jerry and Chaz: Thanks for allowing me the thrill of telling the world what I have learned about God through loving you.

To my Mom: Thank you for being the Proverbs 31

woman in my life. I know Jesus today because I first saw Him in you.

To everyone at Creation House: Rick Nash, for your vision and for giving me this wonderful opportunity; Barbara Dycus, for your dedication to this project; Mark Poulalion and Tameca Nelson, for going the extra mile on the art design

To Charlotte Hale, for your generous contribution and tireless inspiration

To all who shared your stories, the stuff in your lives, so God could use it to bring treasures of hope and encouragement to those who are walking through the hard places.

To my precious sister, Benita Dear; my courageous brothers, Pastor Ben, George Alan, Matt and the rest of the Wade gang; my dear friend and sister-in-law, Ruth Wade

To Danniebelle Hall, my mentor in the ministry

To everyone at Babbie Mason Ministries

To my partner in rhyme and time, Donna I. Douglas

To my student-turned coach, Ann Chastain

To my encourager and friend, Sandy Smith

To my gifted friend, Kenn Mann

To all of you who have touched my life out there on the road: Ashli Carter, Julie Walker-Crews, Belva Kirk, Mary Martha Dabbs, Delia Roman, Adrianne Grant, Yolanda Wilcox and Pastor Jim Cymbala.

Special thanks to those who remain anonymous. It is not necessary to print your name. I know your heart.

Contents

Section II ⤳ GOD'S PROMISES

Section III ⤳ GOD'S PRESENCE

INTRODUCTION

Have you ever been on a stroll through life, minding your own business, when seemingly out of the blue the unexpected happens? Have you ever made plans for your money, your family, your health or your career, when all of a sudden life sneaks up behind you and snatches the rug out from under your feet? The stuff that happens in life is truly unavoidable, even inevitable. But God has fixed it so that life's surprises, even its tragedies, can somehow work together for our good. Whether He takes us over, or whether He takes us through, somehow in it all, we must believe that God is in control of the stuff of life.

God speaks to us in different ways. And it is always profound and amazing. Often, the words from the Bible leap off the page, possessing a life of their own, quickening my heart. I know He wants me to "hear" those words at that very moment. Other times, He speaks through a sermon, a testimony, a song or a conversation with a friend, reminding me that if He did a particular thing for someone else, He can and will do it for me. God works in countless unique and unforgettable ways, teaching us the things He wants us to know. He shows up, right on time, to reveal Himself, sometimes in a new and refreshing way. At other times He comes on the scene, like the loving and familiar Father that He is, and swoops us up into His big arms of protection, delivering us from all danger, seen or unseen.

Those moments, insights and events, usually ordinary and everyday, humorous or profound, surprise, delight and impact us. They stand out as milestones along life's journey. They stay in our minds and hearts, because they testify of God's loving purpose for us.

But just as sure as the long, cold winter follows the warm and colorful Indian summer, the storms of tribulation come along and force us to run for cover. The only Rock that cannot and will not be moved is God, our Teacher, Deliverer and Father. As we burrow into Him for wisdom, shelter and comfort, nuggets of truth are unearthed, wherein He reveals Himself. I call these unearthed truths *Treasures of Heaven in the Stuff of Earth.*

My own heavenly treasures are forged from the stuff of my life's "metal": a Michigan preacher's kid who grew up to become an Atlanta housewife and mother; a teacher who composes Christian music and has the privilege of singing those songs throughout God's world. My stories center around a husband, a home, children, parents, siblings, students, friends and strangers in the checkout line. These nuggets of truth have been unearthed at ordinary times (Little League games, the supermarket, the supper table) and at high moments (a video recording session, the release of a new record project, singing at a Billy Graham Crusade or for the president of the United States).

Compiling and composing these stories has made me

realize that God is always with us. He calls us by name and wants to permeate every facet of our lives. No matter how much or how little we know about Him, God desires for us to know Him even more. Thousands of books have been written, and countless songs have been sung. But we have yet to scratch even the surface of His all-surpassing greatness. In our quest to mine His unsearchable riches, we find that His Word is practical, applicable and able to challenge, correct and change us. At the end of every one of life's lessons, we find *God, the Teacher for every test*, leading us into the bounty of *His principles*.

Wherever we are, God, by His Spirit, is in us. He spurs us on, equipping and encouraging us to press on in spite of adversity. We live in a jaded world that causes us to be leery and skeptical, second-guessing even those we love. But God straightens us up where we are leaning and teaches us to trust His heart, even when we cannot trace His hand. He builds up our faith, increases our trust and safeguards our hopes, assuring us that if He said it, He will surely bring it to pass. Even in our diamond-in-the-rough condition, *God, the Response to every request*, reminds us that our future is as bright as every one of *His promises*.

Whatever the circumstance or occasion, God, our heroic Deliverer, is for us, helping us even when we cannot help ourselves. It is the nature of the beast: Either we find trouble, or trouble finds us. Either way, *God, the Miracle-worker in our mess*, rushes to our aid, slays our enemies and delivers us safely once again. As our relationship with Him deepens, we find that He is more precious than silver and more costly than gold. All the wealth in the world cannot compare to the pleasure of His company. We love Him not just for what He does but for who He is. God, our constant Companion, reminds us once again that we are never out of *His presence*.

Your life, no doubt, is different from mine, but hopefully these stories will resonate with your own experience and stir you to recall the rare lessons or commonplace moments when God revealed His treasure to you. As you delve into these stories, I hope you will be challenged to go on a treasure hunt of your own. Go ahead. Mine and sift through the stuff of your own life. Maybe the treasure is buried, or maybe it's just hidden. I pray that in these stories you will see the power of the Good News of Jesus Christ through the life of this housewife, mother, singer, songwriter, teacher and friend, lovingly cultivated and offered to you, and written to the glory of our Father.

The apostle Paul said it best:

> But we have this treasure in earthen vessels, that the excellence of the power may be of God and not of us. We are hard pressed on every side, yet not crushed; we are perplexed, but not in despair; persecuted, but not forsaken; struck down, but not destroyed—always carrying about in the body the dying of the Lord Jesus, that the life of Jesus also may be manifested in our body . . .
>
> Therefore we do not lose heart. Even though our outward man is perishing, yet the inward man is being renewed day by day. For our light affliction, which is but for a moment, is working for us a far more exceeding and eternal weight of glory, while we do not look at the things which are seen, but at the things which are not seen. For the things which are seen are

temporary, but the things which are not seen are eternal. For we know that if our earthly house, this tent, is destroyed, we have a building from God, a house not made with hands, eternal in the heavens.

—2 CORINTHIANS 4:7–10, 16–18; 5:1

Section I

❧

GOD'S PRINCIPLES

God is always pursuing us, to teach us His ways, to speak to us His truths and to show us His heart. When we hide His Word in our hearts, we find that His Word is practical and able to challenge, correct and change us. When we are faced with life's questions, we will find each answer as God shows up to reveal Himself as the . . .

Teacher for every test.

Chapter 1

MAKING THE MOST OF THE MUNDANE

Recently I flew to Nashville, Tennessee, to shoot a music video. What an awesome, unbelievable opportunity! During the flight, I visualized the upcoming video on television, impacting countless people. I believed in my heart that God would help it become a great video. I prayed He would use it to minister His truth in a medium where lies so often are portrayed.

It can be so easy, I thought, imagining the alluring world of television, *to get caught up in it and subtly, slowly begin to lose one's place.*

When the plane touched down at Music City, a driver met me at the gate, took my baggage claim stub, escorted me to his stretch limousine and then hurried to retrieve my luggage. Like a kid in a candy store, I peered through the window of the limo as we glided through downtown, up Music Row and finally arrived at the studio where I would spend the day singing before the camera.

Soon I was walking onto a storybook-beautiful music set, quickly acquainting myself with its ambiance. Perfect lighting, lavish trails of gauzy backdrops, stately antique furnishings upholstered in rich, red velvet, all softened by the warmth of glowing candles…breathtaking!

The recording company provided an impressive staff for my project. The talented producer mapped out every aspect of the day; the skilled director obviously knew how to call all the shots. After counseling with them, I was ushered to a dressing room where a makeup artist was waiting to begin my makeover. I sat in a tall captain's chair and stared into the mirror as she worked.

Treasure

The mark of a true Christian is not how good we look in our church attire on Sunday, but how well we serve others throughout the week.

Her assistant brought me a cup of herbal tea, then carefully steamed and laid out my wardrobe. All this felt unreal, as if I had suddenly found myself queen for a day. By the time I emerged from the dressing room, transformed, I felt queenly. I had gone in a caterpillar and come out a beautiful butterfly.

Energized and excited, I worked hard all day. Hours later I felt we had achieved a great music video, worthy of any television station in the world where God might want it viewed. I felt grateful and humble as we all talked about its release. After enjoying a nice meal, the limousine wheeled me to the airport and I flew home—first class!

During the short flight home, still dressed in the stylish clothes I'd worn for the filming, I basked in my memories of the day. Eyes closed, I played and replayed the events in my head. But by arrival time in Atlanta, less than an hour later, the fantasy jolted to an abrupt halt. The beat-up suitcase that for years has followed me all over the world awaited me, looking as worn and familiar as old house shoes. Since it has wheels and is easy to maneuver, I didn't need a skycap to carry it to the curb.

I knew my faithful husband awaited me there in his chariot—his pickup truck. Charles had come from the baseball field where he coached a Little League game. His vehicle was loaded with baseball equipment, but I worked my way in among the stuffed canvas bags. It's a familiar routine, one we've fine-tuned through the years. There's no need for Charles to park the car, hike to the gate to meet me and then down to baggage claim and over to the parking garage to pay for parking. It's much simpler to meet me at the curb.

Yes, the fantasy was over. While I buckled up, Charles filled me in with household news. He'd used an insect repellent bomb throughout the house, ridding it of those annoying moths. Tomorrow would be the last day to pay the deposit on our son's trip with the marching band during spring break. The events of my glamorous day faded rapidly into a distant blur.

At home, our thirteen-year-old was still up—more than an hour past his bedtime. He had not taken out the trash. The dishwasher was running, but the sink overflowed with pots and pans from dinner. *The guys in our house at least mean well*, I thought.

I fixed myself a cup of tea, kicked off my high heels and sat down in my peaceful kitchen. Then, out of the corner of my eye, I spotted a long trail of soapy water snaking across the kitchen floor. The dishwasher always floods when dish-washing liquid is used instead of dishwasher crystals. I had to move quickly. Still dressed in the glamour duds I'd worn for the video we'd wrapped up just three hours earlier, I ran to the laundry room, grabbed the mop and began mopping up the soapy water. Never mind the perfect makeup, freshly done fingernails and nicely coiffed hair. I mopped the kitchen floor and did the dirty dishes as only a mother and wife can do them.

People ask me if it's difficult to keep public ministry in per-spective. No, it's not hard to keep all this music artist stuff from going to my head. After a day of singing before thou-sands, signing autographs and hugging necks, I go home to a family of real people—a real husband who is good at slaying flying moths and real kids who play baseball and march in formation among the woodwinds.

Whether pipes burst or the dishwasher overflows, God uses the ordinary incidents to keep me grounded. The stuff of life that happens the moment my feet hit the floor in the morning is the same stuff that keeps me on my knees at night. *If everything were picture perfect,* I tell myself, *I would have no need for God.*

The warmth of the spotlight, applause from the crowd and a Number One hit song look good on the pages of a press kit. But don't tell that to the lady in the green dress on the second pew, who just became a widow. She doesn't care about my awards. At that moment she is looking for a life-line. She needs a word from the Lord. She is praying for a message of hope to take her through her long and lonely nights.

I thank God for the music videos, the Number One hit songs and the wonderful concert opportunities. But I must also find it in my heart to thank God for the flat tire, the lean checking account or even nights spent in the emergency room. Such circumstances keep me dependent on my heavenly Father; He knows the end from the beginning, and He is working it all out together for my good. Those trials allow me to minister out of my own need. I can speak from my own experience, knowing that if God can do it for me, He can do it for the widow in the green dress sitting in the second pew.

After the dishes were done and the floor mopped, I retired for the evening. But not before removing my false eyelashes, press-on nails and lastly, the makeup, which slid slowly down the drain. One glance in the mirror revealed the whole truth.

The girl in the mirror is real. The crow's feet and dark circles under my eyes don't lie. They speak loudly without saying a word. It's as if they say, "Had it not been for the Lord who was on your side, where would you be? You are real, fragile and vulnerable, and God loves you just as you are. God hooked you up the way you are for a purpose. He will help you grow, change and mature into the woman He wants you to be. Embrace every moment."

STUFF

Statistics tell us that the average woman is a size fourteen.

I crawled into bed and snuggled deep into the covers, contented, thankful and relieved. My faithful moth-slaying mate snored contentedly beside me. I whispered a prayer of thanks to

God and asked Him to help me keep my mind stayed on Him.

After all, as a wife and mom with faults and flaws like most others in this world, it's the everyday stuff of life that keeps me grounded and walking close to Him.

Chapter 2

OVER FORTY AND FEELIN' FINE

The year I celebrated my fortieth birthday I received a special birthday card from a friend. It advised me of some things I needed to know once I got "over the hill." Among these things are: I need to be aware that elastic waistbands are essential. I shouldn't look back, or I'll get a stiff neck. Winnebagos will start to look pretty good to me. Don't aspire to become a ballerina. Social Security is running out of money. A mind is a terrible thing to waste, and a waist is a terrible thing to mind.

Author and motivational speaker Mamie McCullough agrees that a woman, at every stage, has a number of needs. She says that between the ages of zero and eighteen a girl needs a good upbringing. Between the ages of eighteen and twenty-five a girl needs a good education. Between the ages of twenty-five and forty-five a girl needs a good occupation. Between the ages of forty-five and sixty-five a girl needs a nice home. At sixty-five and older a girl needs cash!

In our society lots of people make jokes about turning forty. But turning forty isn't nearly as bad as it seems. Since I turned forty I've developed a lot more than a few wrinkles. I've developed a few other choice qualities, too. Take *confidence,* for example. I am what you call a full-figured girl. I'd rather call myself and women like me...*real women.* Statistics say that the average woman is a size fourteen. Women today have been conditioned to think that beauty and anorexia are synonymous.

It's easy for us to compare ourselves to...*her.* There *she* is. We see *her* on television every day. *She* is half my age and five inches taller than I am. *She* has perfect hair, beautiful skin and nails and wants to lose five pounds so *she* can get into a size six before summer. Come on. Give me a break! Some part of me wants to reach inside the television set and grab *her* by the nape of the neck and say, "Come on into the real world where the real women live, honey." But another thing women over forty must have is *control!*

Treasure

We never get a failing grade in God's school of faith.

In my younger days, too often I struggled with the need to compete—to keep up with or surpass the accomplishments of my friends and colleagues. I was driven to stay in the fast lane. I was motivated by the stuff that comes along with working hard: recognition, awards, financial gain. Along the way, I garnered a few earthly treasures and trophies. In the process I found that the best things in life are not *things.* Here in this new season of confidence, I've discovered a sense of rest, having little left to prove to myself except for an increased need to know more of Christ.

After some years of buffing, another choice quality is beginning to shine through. That quality is *contentment.* Like the good ol' philosopher Popeye said, "I yam what I yam. That's all I yam." I agree with Popeye. Like him, I have learned to accept myself for who I am and be satisfied.

But that didn't happen overnight. A few years ago, just a few months prior to my fortieth birthday, I was privileged to sing at a conference in Hawaii. I took a favorite girlfriend with me. We were having a great time enjoying the island until she announced that we couldn't leave without going to the beach. Now, I'm a pretty confident person, and I am learning to be content, but I wasn't crazy about the idea of putting these hips into a swimsuit! I mean, I had not been in a swimsuit in public since my gym class in the seventh grade. I wasn't about to come out of hiding on the beautiful beaches of Hawaii.

However, it dawned on me that if I didn't overcome this fear and insecurity, it would surely overcome me. I wasn't about to let that happen. So I went shopping, bought a swimsuit and went to the beach. For the first time in my life I snorkeled to my heart's delight. It was one of the most memorable experiences I've ever had. Exploring God's beautiful underwater world was breathtaking. And I found that there were many people on the beach with much more interesting figures than mine.

That experience was a turning point for me. The world whispers into my ear and says, *"If you want to be successful you've got to be young, thin, blond, single and white."* Where does that leave an older, married, African American mother of two—with hips? Right where God wants me. He wants me to just keep on showing up for work.

For the past sixteen years, the Lord has blessed me with a wonderful music ministry that has taken me around the world. But for most of these years, I had been a slave to my calendar. So I made a *commitment* to myself to lead a more sensible life. The word *no* comes a lot more frequently these days. Children turn into teenagers, and time is no longer an ally. Every mother wants to raise her children and be involved in every area of their lives. Every woman finds it necessary to work on her marriage. I've said humorously for years that I needed strength and wisdom to train up my husband in the way he should go, so that when he is old he will not depart from it. If you are married, then you will agree that you have to be home to do that. Every believer wants to be involved in the life of her church. You must be connected to benefit from that. And every girl needs the companionship of a few close friends. Even though I am a long way from retiring, it sure does feel good to have a little more balance in my life.

I've often thought that all those references to the number forty in the Bible were more than just coincidence. I was right. It rained forty days and nights. God looked for forty righteous men in Sodom. The Israelites wandered in the desert for forty years. Moses was on Mount Sinai forty days and nights when he received the Ten Commandments. Jesus fasted forty days and nights in the wilderness before entering the ministry. These are just a few examples.

According to the Bible, *forty* is a number that suggests probation, testing, separation or judgment. Can you identify with that definition? Do you feel that your life has been one big test? Maybe circumstances have left you feeling like a student who is made to stay after school. You feel that you have been assigned to write your lesson over and over until you get it right. God is patient. We never get a failing grade in God's school of faith.

All our years thus far have been a succession of challenges revealing what we are really made of. Circumstances that tried our faith have stretched us, showing how pliable we are in God's hands and exposing our true character. Tests we've taken along the way reveal our resilience. The hills we've climbed and crested expose

STUFF

What is the one dream that you would fulfill if you had no mental or physical boundaries and unlimited funds? What is keeping you from fulfilling that dream?

our weaknesses, but they also display our ability to endure. The bumps and bruises we've sustained portray our tenacious spirit—the spirit that says, like the old gospel song, "We've come this far by faith, leaning on the Lord."

If what goes up must come down, then what goes in must come out. After the fortieth day or fortieth year in the wilderness, there was a coming out. The years after forty are our coming-out years! We've been tested and tried in the fires of life. What does testing do? It refines and burns away impurities. The Book of Job, a book that talks a lot about testing, also talks about wisdom. Job 12:12 says, "Wisdom is with aged men, and with length of days, understanding." Job

23:10 says, "But He knows the way that I take; when He has tested me, I shall come forth as gold."

Women who have walked with God know that He has established a flawless track record. If He delivered us before, He'll do it again. As our relationship with God matures, we realize that what used to alarm us doesn't shake us as it used to. We are learning our lessons. You see, God went with us into our wilderness experience, and He will bring us out into our promised land. Women over forty must learn to exercise their faith muscles. I believe that God has built into us an innate ability to trust Him and believe for the possible in impossible situations.

Women over forty must not buy into the lie that says we're too old. Too weak. Too fat. Too thin. Not pretty enough. Not smart enough. Underqualified. Overqualified. Insignificant. Too opinionated. Too stiff. Too fragile. God begs to differ with man's opinions. Remember, we matter to God at every age and every stage of life. Romans 12:2 reminds us in these powerful words: "Do not be conformed to this world, but be transformed by the renewing of your mind, that you may prove what is that good and acceptable and perfect will of God."

If you are forty years or older, I have a homework assignment to give you. If you haven't arrived there yet, try the assignment anyway, or pass it on to your mother, sister or friend. This exercise will pump you up with encouragement and remind you that God is not even close to being finished with you. It is meant to challenge you to color outside of the lines, so to speak. Try some new things, maybe for the first time.

Today, start making a list of all the "first things" that you have done since you turned forty. For example, since I turned forty I have:

- Written my first book
- Written my first musical
- Won my first pair of Dove Awards (the gospel music equivalent to the Grammy)
- Had my first pedicure
- Caught my biggest fish (a thirty-seven-pound king salmon)
- Sent my first son to college and celebrated with him when he received his degree
- Gone parasailing—not once, but three times
- Delivered my first commencement address
- Met my first president of the United States
- Hosted my first radio and television programs
- Taken my first mission trip to a Third World country
- Completed my first 10K road race
- Harvested my first vegetable garden
- Taught my first class on a college campus

Remember that God has a plan for your *entire* life. Your best years are yet to come. As Jeremiah 29:11 says, "'For I know the plans I have for you,' declares the Lord, 'plans to prosper you and not to harm you, plans to give you hope and a future'" (NIV). These are your coming-out years. Celebrate them with your own coming-out party. If your friends threw a mock funeral for you when you turned forty, celebrate your fortieth again. Throw a big party and wear bold colors. Don't just celebrate for one day. Celebrate the entire month.

Then encourage yourself in the Lord. Tell yourself, "I'm coming out. I'm not coming out the way I went in. I'm coming out a different way—changed. I'm coming out of my old way of thinking. I'm coming out of debt. I'm putting aside old ideas and stereotypes. I'm doing away with old attitudes and habits. I'm turning over a new leaf. I'm starting a new chapter. Today is a brand-new day."

Chapter 3

❧

A GOOD SERVANT
IS HARD TO FIND

D r. Paul L. Walker, general international overseer for the Church of God, Cleveland, Tennessee, once spoke these eloquent words at the funeral of my dear friend's mother. "Man has learned to transmit his voice across paper-thin wires to communicate with someone else on the other side of the globe. Man has learned to use a scalpel to operate between the beats of a heart. But one great lesson man has failed to learn is the lesson on how to be a servant. If you aim to be a great leader, you will always be disappointed. People don't want to be led. But if you desire to be a great servant, you will never be disappointed."

The Lord reminded me not long ago of what a real servant looks like through the life of someone I easily took for granted when I was younger. I will not soon forget this lesson—or the servant God used to teach it.

Thedora Lewis was my Sunday school teacher. For as long as I knew her, she was old. Her wavy, white hair was never done up in professionally coiffed curls, but was always braided. Her nails were never manicured or painted in pretty colors. Though neatly dressed, she never wore the latest fashions. She never showed even the slightest bit of makeup on her reddish-brown skin. Her glasses were outdated. She never married or had children. She lived alone. I never knew her to have many friends. She seldom ventured away from our hometown, unless she was with our church on an outing.

Once our congregation attended a huge national conference. Theodora came along as a member of the delegation. Not one to take risks, she held up traffic at the top of an escalator because she was too hesitant to step onto the moving stairs. After long deliberation and some coaxing from my father, her pastor, she took the big step and went for the wild ride downward. Thedora didn't lead a very exciting life outside of our church.

Treasure

If you aim to be a great leader, you will always be disappointed. People don't want to be led. But if you aim to be a great servant, you will never be disappointed.

As our youth Sunday school teacher, Thedora taught all my brothers, my sister and me, a volunteer position that spanned more than three decades. I remember that our class of prepubescent grade-schoolers was often unruly. She did well to teach us the golden text from the Sunday school lesson without interruption. But to my remembrance, she never missed a Sunday.

Thedora also sang in the choir. Well, to say she sang is perhaps being kind. She was present in the choir. She had a voice that sang an octave too low, was a measure behind and was always out of tune. But she was *present and accounted for* at every choir rehearsal and worship service, come rain or shine, with a purse full of cough drops, ready and willing to come to the aid of any choir member who showed the slightest signs of laryngitis. Every Sunday morning, without fail, she donned her freshly pressed choir robe and was at her post, ready for the choir's processional at the stroke of eleven.

Thedora often made craft items for our family. She crocheted rugs from plastic bags or made trivets from used Popsicle sticks. Each time she presented one of her gifts, her simple gesture somehow spoke volumes. She gave one of her small gifts to my mother one Sunday. Mother still hides this precious memory in her heart. The gift was a pencil with an eraser at both ends. Scripted on the pencil were these words: "Life without Jesus Christ is like this pencil. It has no point."

Thedora Lewis died well into her eighties. Her funeral was the only time in my father's forty-year pastorate when he did not preach a eulogy. He said Thedora Lewis powerfully preached her own funeral by the faithful life she lived.

What a legacy she left us. Thedora Lewis is still teaching, although she graduated to heaven nearly two decades ago. Her life taught me that it is not important to live a life filled with great means, but to live a life filled with great meaning. Her simple existence demonstrated that it is far better to be faithful than to be fashionable. To our ears, she may not have been a great singer. But I truly believe God was more pleased with her joyful noise, sung with a heart full of gratitude, than He was with those who had beautiful voices but sang begrudgingly. She was, by every measure, a servant who was faithful to keep showing up for work. She wasn't the greatest teacher, but she preached a sermon every day of her life. That sermon still resounds today. Her example taught her students and fellow church members that the mark of a true Christian is not how good we look in our church attire on Sunday, but how well we serve others throughout the week.

Jesus, the Master Servant, taught His disciples a great lesson on service in Mark 9:35: "If anyone desires to be first, he must be last of all and servant of all." In God's economy, the one who is the least is the one who is the greatest. Jesus, from His very first breath as a baby in a barnyard manger to His very last breath as the Savior at Calvary, exhibited the life of a servant.

Genuine servants are those who know it's not necessary to have great talent or financial resources in order to be used. They just show up, in obedience, with whatever is in their hand. The widow from Zarephath in 1 Kings 17 had a handful of flour in the jar and a little oil in the bottle when the prophet Elijah arrived on her doorstep and asked her to prepare him a meal. Verse 15 says she did what she was asked to do, and she, the prophet Elijah and her son ate for many days. God delights in and rewards those who bring their gifts to Him in faith and obedience.

It's just like God to use the simplest thing to confound man's sophisticated ways of reasoning and rationalizing. In the Gospel of John, Jesus uses a little boy's lunch of two small fish and five small loaves of bread to feed a multitude of five thousand very hungry people (6:9–13). It's not about the gift; it's about what the Giver can do with it. Whether sitting in a house in Zarephath, distributing five thousand fish sandwiches to a very hungry multitude on a hillside or teaching children in a Sunday school class, little is much when God is in it.

Great singers and great orators are easy to find. People with talent are every-where. But a great servant is a rare and precious jewel. Real servants teach us more by what they do than by what they say. They give of what is in their hearts as well as what is in their hands. Without servants to warm us with

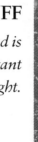

STUFF

Being kind is more important than being right.

their gracious deeds that often go unappreciated, the world would be a much colder place. Horace Trauble said it best, "If the world is cold, make it your business to build fires."

Chapter 4

❧

MIRACLE CHILD

This story begins around 1948 with a young Black couple from Sunflower, Mississippi. The man had survived World War II, despite several brushes with death. While serving overseas, God had called him to preach the gospel.

The girl, who married the young soldier shortly after both graduated from high school, saw her parents move north during a great migration of others seeking work opportunities. When the couple and their small son followed her parents, they lived at first in a boarding house with other Black families while the husband found a job at the Goodyear tire factory.

Life improved. A second son arrived. Soon after, the young wife became pregnant again. The full-term, apparently healthy baby girl arrived on a cold February day, and the joyous parents

Treasure

All I have seen has taught me to trust the Creator for all I have not seen.
—Ralph Waldo Emerson

took her home from the hospital a few days later.

Soon, however, the couple noticed with alarm that their newborn's eyes did not seem to focus. Worse, her tiny head had begun to swell. The parents felt apprehensive. Their doctor could not relieve their fears. His diagnosis—hydrocephalus—was frightening: *water on the brain*. Operations could help, but no one could predict or guarantee the outcome. Whatever the potential for damage, the fluid must be drained from the brain. The infant was scheduled for surgery.

STUFF

Woman-to-woman stuff— Somewhere in this audience may even be someone who will one day follow in my footsteps and preside over the White House as the president's spouse. I wish him well!
—Barbara Bush
Wellesley College commencement address, 1990

In a situation where most parents might feel helpless and overwhelmed, this couple swung into action. By now the resolute young father had begun pastoring a small group of believers. His baby church rallied to the need, with members praying diligently for the child's life and health. They especially prayed about the shunt that soon must be surgically inserted in the skull to drain excess fluids away from the brain.

One surgery, then another, helped relieve fluid pressure. As they waited for their child to become old enough and strong enough to sustain the delicate operation to install a shunt, the parents prayed. The church prayed. The child grew.

Prior to that most critical surgery, however, doctors found themselves confounded. The girl was walking, talking and laughing. She had become a happy, lively toddler. It seemed nearly impossible that this healthy-looking baby must undergo the risky procedure.

Incredibly, doctors discovered the shunt was not needed. All swelling and excess fluids were gone. Equally important was the fact that amazingly the child's brain obviously functioned fully and normally. Except for the surgical scar beneath her dark curls, no trace of hydrocephalus could be found.

I, Babbie Mason, was that baby. Even as a young child, I could feel that scar tissue and recognize with awe that God had saved my life. It took years, however, for me to fully appreciate what great things He had done.

For starters, my parents never received a bill for the skillful surgery, which, prior to present-day imaging techniques, always represented a life-threatening procedure. The consummate medical skills bestowed on me restored me to fully functioning life, yet my parents never knew who paid the bill or who donated such exquisite care. They always marveled at the goodness of God, who had His hand on their daughter from the moment of her birth, and even before.

Throughout my early life, many people told me how they had prayed for me and rejoiced to see the "miracle baby" grow and thrive. I grew up understanding that God had His hand on my life. I could touch my head and feel a tactile reminder of Him. The long scar reminds me that God's grace is in operation, the pain is gone and healing has taken place.

As an adult, I sometimes feel that scar and realize the evil one had determined to destroy my brain—that part of me that thinks, feels and directs all my actions. He wanted to destroy the thoughts, ideas, songs and talents of a tiny baby God had selected, even then, to serve Him.

Our God is mighty to save. As Paul wrote, He is "able to do exceedingly abundantly above all that we ask or think" (Eph. 3:20).

Are you up against an impossible situation? Ask God for the miracle you need. Thank Him for the miracles you have received. He is a miracle-working God, and I have a scar that proves it.

Chapter 5

BALANCING ACT

As a gospel singer, God blesses my husband and me with extraordinary opportunities to worship with believers all over the world, in many different settings. I'm always fascinated by the various ways in which the body of Christ worships.

Some churches are extremely free and emotional, with lots of singing and shouting. Others are quiet and conservative, with very structured worship styles. Some churches sing hymns; others sing gospel choruses. Some churches focus on evangelism; others focus on personal growth. Some clap on beats one and three, others on beats two and four. Many do not clap at all.

I grew up in a Black Baptist church, where my father was pastor and I was the church pianist. We considered worship a verb. From its onset, each service throbbed with life and action. We clapped our hands and tapped our feet. We agreed with the preaching by adding "amen!" It seemed that everything was loud. The singing was loud. Preaching was loud. Music was loud.

Our worship services lasted well into the afternoon—with no thought of the time. My father began by reading from his chosen Bible text. He was a great teacher, with deep insight into the Word of God. As he developed each point, the congregation encouraged him. As he preached and exhorted, his voice would rise, and with each point in his sermon, the congregation increased its fervor.

Toward the end, my father preached as if his message were a song. When he took a breath, the organ filled in the blank. The congregation sang their "amens" and "hallelujahs" back to him in a rhythmic pulse that gradually crescendoed into shouts. If our church had anything, it had spirit! But sometimes, by the end of the service, there was so much spirit you could no longer hear the preaching.

Then I went off to college and discovered, at a Southern Michigan conservative Christian liberal arts school, a totally different kind of worship experience. The congregation there sang the great old hymns of the faith exactly as they were written in the hymnal. The musicians played only the original score, and not a note more. Services were quiet, worshipful and dignified. They never deviated from the order of worship. The pastor preached the truth from God's Word with great eloquence, and you could hear every word with no distractions.

There was plenty of opportunity to agree with the preaching, but no one dared to clap their hands, pat their feet or say "amen." Services were dismissed in precisely one hour and fifteen minutes. If there was one element sure to be found in those services, it was truth. But even on that beautiful campus, sometimes the truth seemed difficult to endure, even for an hour.

In John 4:24 we're told, "God is Spirit, and those who

worship Him must worship in spirit *and* truth" (emphasis added). Jesus encourages us to worship with our heads and our hearts. If we focus only on the spirit, we may feel good, but we cannot always trust our feelings to enable us to make good decisions. Likewise, if we focus only on truth, we may have an intellectual experience, but little joy.

Treasure

The Word without the Spirit ... we dry up. The Spirit without the Word ... we blow up. But when the Word and the Spirit are working together, we grow up.

I often compare a balanced church to a peanut butter-and-jelly sandwich. Some churches focus only on truth. Truth, like peanut butter, is chock-full of vitamins. If you were marooned on a desert island with nothing to eat but peanut butter, you could survive. But peanut butter by itself can be bland and boring. It sticks to the roof of your mouth. It becomes dry and hard to swallow.

Other churches focus mainly on the Spirit. Worship service must be exciting, the music joyful, the responses filled with emotion. Like jelly, those worship experiences can be lacking in substances—a sweet experience for the moment, but nothing to live on throughout the week. Too much of this leads to a malnourished, out-of-balance body.

Mix the two together, however, and serve with fresh bread and a tall glass of milk, and you have one of mankind's favorite meals. When the main ingredients, Spirit and truth, are blended together and served with the Bread of Life, who is Christ, it is ready to nourish a hungry world—a world starving to know the love of God and desperately needing the pure spiritual milk of God's Word.

The Bible likens the church to the human body. Like the human body, the church has many parts, each designed to do a specific job. Large or small, each cell, organ and vessel play an important role in keeping the body running efficiently. Just as a balanced diet keeps the physical body healthy, the body of Christ must exercise balance in worship to meet the needs of the church and the world.

In John 4:24 Jesus told the woman at the well that true worshipers "must worship in spirit and truth." Spirit and truth must operate together. I heard a preacher use this powerful illustration: "The Word without the Spirit... we dry up. The Spirit without the Word...we blow up. But when the Word and the Spirit are working together, we grow up."

STUFF

The chance of bread falling with the peanut butter-and-jelly side down is directly proportionate to the cost of the carpet.

—Murphy's Law

Most of us have looked at worship from one of these viewpoints. Is your own personal worship out of balance? Ask God to help you discover a new dimension in worship as you prayerfully seek the right balance of Spirit and truth in your life.

Chapter 6

DON'T LIE TO YOUR MOMMA

There's a story making the rounds that makes me chuckle. It seems a young man and his female roommate invited his mother over for dinner.

Now the mother, suspicious of this male-female arrangement, felt extra concern as she watched her son relate to the pretty young thing. As she watched the two over the course of the evening, John's momma felt more and more certain she didn't like the situation.

"I know what you're thinking," her son told her, "but let me assure you that Julie and I are just roommates."

A week later, Julie asked John about a missing piece of her silver service. "Ever since your mother's visit, I can't seem to find that beautiful silver gravy ladle," she remarked. "You don't suppose she took it, do you?"

"I doubt it," John replied, "but I'll write a letter to

Treasure

He is a fool to leave behind things close at hand to follow what is out of reach.
—Plutarch

Mom to make sure." His letter read:

> Dear Mother,
> I'm not saying you did take the gravy ladle from the house, and I'm not saying you did not take it. I am saying, however, that it has been missing since you came to dinner.
>
>   Love, John

STUFF

Policies are many; principles are few. Policies may change; principles never do.

Several days later, John received a reply from his mother. She wrote:

> Dear Son,
> I'm not saying you do sleep with Julie, and I'm not saying you do not. I am saying, however, that if she were sleeping in her own bed, she would have found the gravy ladle by now.
>
>   Love, Mom

Lesson of the day: DON'T LIE TO YOUR MOM.

Chapter 7

HAVING DONE ALL ... STAND!

Some of the most valuable life lessons I have learned were taught by my mother. In terms of faith, endurance and resilience, my mother is the most solid woman I know—one who maintains great dignity and exudes quiet strength. I have watched her stand strong in the face of adversity ... especially since my father's passing.

During recent years without Dad, my mother has stayed the course, trusting God always, even at those times when there seemed to be no answers. Her secret is simple. Once, addressing an audience of women, she said people often tried to comfort her by encouraging her to "hang in there."

Never at a loss for words, Mom shared her own unique interpretation of that phrase—and her words encouraged me more than most sermons I've heard!

"You could hang in there," my mother said. "But you don't *want* to hang in there. When you're *hanging*, you're out of control, dangling by a thread, holding on for dear life. You are vulnerable to your circumstances.

"To hang in there is to be like a sheet on your grand-mother's clothesline, exposed to rain, dust and other elements that can sneak up behind it and take it by surprise.

The neighbor's children could run through the yard, snatching the sheet to the ground and leaving it ruined.

"It's not good to be in a hanging position. The only picture I can conjure up is that of a noose. So you don't ever want to hang! It means you have no course of action, just a neutral position, relinquishing all control. When you're in spiritual warfare, this mind-set can mean certain death!

"Instead, as Ephesians 6:13–14 says, 'Therefore take up the whole armor of God, that you may be able to withstand in the evil day, and having done all, to stand. Stand, therefore...'

"So," my mother concluded, "you don't ever want to just hang in there. Jesus Christ was hung up for our hang-ups so we could stand up, firm and strong, on the promises in His Word!"

Those thoughts came from a woman who raised five children, an old-fashioned, strict disciplinarian. She didn't resort to such contemporary discipline techniques as counting to three or time-outs. Mom spoke once, and that was it. We complied, or we suffered the consequences. She said what she meant and meant what she said, and she did it all with unconditional love. Mom was firm, and I don't see where I or my siblings suffered from it.

The embodiment of the Proverbs 31 woman, my mother's abilities could make the average woman jealous. Beautiful on the outside, a perfect hostess, homemaker and cook, she also can do almost anything with her hands—seamstress, angler, plumber, carpenter—you name it. She personifies the successful pastor's wife, having worked alongside my father for nearly forty years. As a mentor to younger women and older women alike, she put feet to her prayers, and served in almost every church capacity from janitor to Bible study teacher to church organist and choir director.

Yes, Mom always has done so much more than just hang in there. Our home overflowed with music, and her melodious voice no doubt became my greatest, earliest musical influence. She was always singing as she cleaned, cooked or prepared for church. I am grateful to God that we sing together now. She made guest appearances on two of my recordings, and she travels with me at times. Certainly, her voice and her life are rich treasures.

Treasure

Courage is fear that has said its prayers.
—Karie Wilson Baker

My mother's advice—"Don't just hang in there, but STAND"—has carried me through some tough times. I hope her words offer you strength to forge through tough times of your own. The forces of the enemy are very real, but God has provided us with every weapon needed to make us more than conquerors.

From head to toe, He has equipped us for battle. He gave us the belt of truth so we can remain established in the face of error and never waver. He dressed us with the breastplate of righteousness so we can stand against lawlessness and injustice. He placed our feet on a sure foundation, enabling us to carry the good news of the gospel into a dark and chaotic world. The shield of faith protects us from the flaming arrows of the enemy. The helmet of salvation is ours as we experience God's sure deliverance. God has armed us with the sword of the Spirit, which is the Word of God, empowering us to keep our enemies at bay.

Notice, however, that God's armor covers only the front. He does not intend for us to cower and run, allowing the enemy to take potshots at our rear.

So take it from the apostle Paul—and my mother. After you've done all you know how to do, don't hang in there. Keep standing. After you have prayed all you know how to pray and cried until there are no more tears, STAND FIRM.

When there is too much month and too little money, STAND. If people promised they'd be there when the going got tough, but left you alone and holding the bag, establish yourself. When the only certainty in your life is uncertainty and the bottom is dropping out from beneath you, keep standing.

Then, God's people discover that when you get to the bottom, you will find the bottom is firm and secure, and you will still be able to stand the principles and promises of God's Word.

STUFF

Approximately four million Americans suffer from generalized anxiety disorder. Sufferers are known to agonize over money, health, family, work or other topics— even when there is no sign of trouble.

Chapter 8

~

KEEP IT SIMPLE, SISTER

When dinner is over, I love to gather the family and oftentimes friends around the dining table to play games—especially a word game called Taboo. As a writer, I always find word games fun and challenging.

With Taboo, the goal is to get your teammates to say a word that is printed at the top of a small card. The bottom of the card, however, lists certain words you cannot use as clues. While your team wildly guesses words from the description you gave them, they are racing against sand running through an egg timer. Each person on your team gets a card, and the first team who reaches a score of fifty points wins the game.

I love this game, so when my turn came I quickly glanced at the key word and then at the words I couldn't use. I proceeded to prod my teammates. "This is an occupation. These people use hammer and nails, screwdrivers and screws, and they erect things." My team stared at me blankly and shouted a few wild guesses.

"They pour concrete," I added. "When it rains, they lay a tarp on the roof. They install things. They have crews of electricians and plumbers."

"A Sears repairman!" someone yelled out.

I felt frustrated. Such a common word, and I couldn't get my team to say it. Then the time ran out, and my turn was over.

Then Ashli, a precious little eight-year-old on our team, bounced around to look at the word I couldn't get our team to say. Ashli is smart as a whip and cute as a button. Confidently looking around at everyone else, she asked, "What job did Jesus have in the Bible?"

"A carpenter!" everyone called out in unison.

I placed Ashli's cute little face in my hands and gave her a big kiss on the forehead. There I was, a writer by profession, struggling, digging deep into my descriptive vocabulary to evoke the correct response from my team...and failing.

Meanwhile Ashli, an excellent student, took a far more direct approach. In a few simple words, she communicated the right idea to everyone.

Isn't it amazing how adult Christians complicate things? We learn the fundamental teachings of God's Word, then somewhere down the line add our own beliefs, mixed with a dash of personal philosophy, and create our own principles and doctrines. For example, take the subject of Christ's return. Whether pretribulation, midtribulation or posttribulation, the church has argued and speculated for generations. Lengthy discourses are supposed to prove our various claims, yet the bottom line remains that Jesus is coming *soon*.

The Bible puts it plainly:

> But concerning the times and the seasons, brethren, you have no need that I should write to you. For you yourselves know perfectly that the day of the Lord so

comes as a thief in the night.

—1 THESSALONIANS 5:1–2

Entire denominations have been founded on differences in thought. Such issues as "once saved, always saved" or whether a man can "fall from grace" have split denominations and churches for centuries.

The wonderful, simple truth, however, is that if you call upon the name of the Lord, you will be saved. In fact, the gospel message is simple enough for a little child to understand and tell.

Treasure

K.I.S.S.–*Keep it simple, sister! Keep it simple, sir!*

Jesus used a child to illustrate to His disciples the futility of arguing about who would be greatest in God's kingdom. Matthew 18:2–4 tells how Jesus called a little child to stand beside Him, and then said these words: "Assuredly, I say to you, unless you are converted and become as little children, you will by no means enter the kingdom of heaven. Therefore whoever humbles himself as this little child is the greatest in the kingdom of heaven."

My little teammate Ashli taught me a simple but valuable lesson that day. Compare our clue-giving techniques. Mine were so lengthy, wordy and confusing that nobody knew where I was heading; Ashli's were simple, direct and easy to understand. She even went straight to the Bible for a great illustration.

Like Ashli, we need to realize that the message of the gospel is not complicated. The Bible tells about a brilliant man named Nicodemus who knew much about Jewish laws. He came to Jesus to learn how he could enter the kingdom of heaven. Jesus answered very simply: "You must be born again."

We can imagine Jesus speaking to sophisticated Nicodemus as simply as He would speak to Ashli, showing Nicodemus during that life-changing encounter that the kingdom of God involves not a set of laws, but a personal decision.

Nicodemus learned that God's love does not discriminate against others, but draws everyone in. God's love is not self-centered, but self-sacrificing, giving instead of taking. The kingdom of heaven exists not for the religious, but for any who desire a vibrant relationship with our Lord Jesus Christ.

STUFF

*Stuff to think about—
What is one thing you
dislike about yourself?
What can you do to
change it?*

God's kingdom never tears down, but always builds up. For you, me, Ashli and Nicodemus, it really is not complicated. The profound yet simple message is this:

> For God so loved the world that He gave His only begotten Son, that whoever believes in Him should not perish but have everlasting life.
>
> —JOHN 3:16

We need to communicate the love of Christ to the people in our world, and we must learn not to complicate it. Those who hunger and thirst for God and His love will understand our message better if we allow Jesus to choose our words—and keep them simple.

Chapter 9

OPPOSITES ATTACK

Charles and I are total personality opposites. My husband grew up in the country in a middle-Alabama settlement so remote that people don't tell you the town they're from—they tell you the county they are from.

I was raised in the city; Charles grew up as much under the care of his rural grandparents as the care of his mother. He comes from a very loving family and is the product of strict, old-time virtues. Eleven years older than I, he is an old-fashioned, common-sense person who is not easily impressed by "book sense."

I, however, am a schoolteacher and a progressive thinker; I am very attached to books and the arts. Where Charles likes wrestling, fishing and getting his hands dirty, I love fashion. I enjoy a nice car; Charles loves his old, beat-up pickup truck.

So we're very different. In fact, when we were first married we hardly ever agreed on anything. Difficulties soon arose. One thing I particularly criticized about my husband then was the way he misused the language. For example, soon after we were married I told him, "Charles Mason, I love you so much."

"The feeling is *neutral*," he replied.

"Charles, I think the word is *mutual*," the schoolteacher in me instructed him. "Repeat after me: The feeling is mutual."

He'd get so frustrated when I'd correct him that way. In a prayer meeting he requested prayer for a friend with "cancer of the pantry." I knew he meant "pancreas."

Treasure

An English professor wrote the words "woman without her man is nothing" on the blackboard and instructed the students to punctuate it correctly. The men wrote: "Woman, without her man, is nothing." The women wrote: "Woman! Without her, man is nothing."

This went on for years. Charles would misuse a word; I'd correct him. He would get frustrated, and it made both of us unhappy. Problems multiplied in our marriage.

Then the Lord allowed what seemed to be a stumbling block to become a stepping stone. Our teenage son had violated his curfew by fifteen or twenty minutes on two successive Saturday nights, so on the following weekend Charles announced that if it happened again, he intended to have a chat with the young man. I decided to wait up and keep the peace.

Jerry came in a little late. Charles met him at the door, sat him down and said, "Son, this week you're not going outside, not having any company and not talking on the phone.

"You'll do your homework, do your chores and you'll go to bed. In other words, you're on *prescription*."

Jerry and I looked at each other. Then, we couldn't hold back. It struck us so funny that we fell on the floor laughing. Charles, who meant to say "restriction," had no clue as to why we were laughing. Needless to say, the laughter subsided, but the punishment remained.

But for the first time, I saw humor in what had irritated me for years. From then on I'd allow myself to chuckle whenever Charles came up with one of his verbal near misses. Very distinctly, God began to show me that a word or two might be a mistake, but *Charles* is no mistake. God had made him exactly as he is for a purpose. Further, I have come to see that part of his charm is the way he is—verbal misses and all.

Now if Charles misuses a word, it seems delightful. And as I look at our long list of personality differences, I see them as part of God's plan. In ministry, our different roles become very necessary. While I pursue the creative side, Charles oversees the business part. He is very adept and astute, possessing not only good ethics but also excellent business sense. I can trust him absolutely and relax, knowing that whereas other recording artists have to pay hefty agent fees, Charles is so talented he can do such work in-house.

STUFF

*Funny stuff—
The future ain't
what it used to be.
—Yogi Berra*

Today, if my husband utters the wrong word, I can chuckle, and we both can laugh together. In a Wal-Mart store

(Charles pronounces it "Wal-Mark") recently, he saw a man wearing a Promise Keeper's cap. Charles was wearing his cap too, so the two men paused to compare notes about a recent conference.

"It was great," the White brother commented. Charles agreed. "It was a wonderful worship experiment." I didn't have to say "experience" under my breath—or say anything at all. I just silently smiled and enjoyed him. His precious way of looking at life gives me much joy. His unique self, so different from me, is something God has taught me not to try to change, but to love and appreciate more each year we are married.

Opposites can learn from one another—or they can learn to attack one another. So as I recall the last time we were in a restaurant and Charles ordered "a seizure salad, with extra coupons, topped with Caucasian chicken," and I knew he really meant to say Caesar salad, with extra croutons, topped with Cajun chicken, I smile and use our son's "prescription" as a prescription for healthy change.

Chapter 10

FIFTEEN ITEMS OR LESS

Ilove the grocery store express lane. It's meant for people on a mission. It's designed for those who have places to go, things to do and not a lot of time in which to do them.

You see, grocery shopping is not my favorite sport. It's too time consuming. First, I must check our kitchen cupboards and make a list. Then I must carve out an hour or so to complete the task. Afterward, I must load the car. Often, after I shop for enough food to last our family for a week or so, I'll exit the store to discover a downpour in the parking lot. Grocery shopping can be a hassle.

But a recent trip was different. I didn't need a cart for the two items I'd picked up. The line at the express lane was short, only a few people ahead of me, each holding only one or two items. It felt good to know that in just moments I'd be out of that store and on my way.

In the express lane to my left, however, I spotted a woman pushing a cart overflowing with produce, meats, breads and cereal—she had enough food to feed a family of six for a week!

I was appalled. How dare this woman get in the express lane! I was glad I was not behind her, because I might have given her a piece of my mind. Couldn't she read? Didn't she know that the express lane is for people in a hurry? The sign above her head plainly read, "Express Lane. Fifteen items of less."

How rude of her!

After I quickly handed the cashier in my lane my two little items, I glanced over at the next lane, shaking my head disapprovingly as the lady unloaded her heaped-up grocery cart.

Treasure

Many times the problem with Christians is that we are overexposed and underdeveloped.

My purchases came to less than ten dollars. Reaching for my wallet and the ten-dollar bill I thought I had, I discovered I had no cash. "I'll have to write a check," I told the cashier. She gave me a disgusted smirk, rolled her eyes toward the sign above my head and said, "Can't you read? This line is *cash only*."

My embarrassment rose even higher when she added, "Yes, you may write a check *this time*," in a voice clearly audible way back to the meat department. She had to summon a manager to approve my check. I could feel the restless, muttering customers behind me in line, ready to barbecue me at the stake. At last the manager came and approved my check, and I could hurry out of the store.

I don't know about that other woman who didn't read the Express Lane sign, but I do know the Holy Spirit began dealing with me before I reached the parking lot. I could hear some words from Matthew ringing in my head. Though I couldn't recall all of that passage, I knew the essence of the message. That night, I looked it up.

> Judge not, that you be not judged. For with what judgment you judge, you will be judged; and with the measure you use, it will be measured back to you. And why do you look at the speck in your brother's eye, but do not consider the plank in your own eye? Or how can you say to your brother, "Let me remove the speck from your eye"; and look, a plank is in your own eye? Hypocrite! First remove the plank from your own eye, and then you will see clearly to remove the speck from your brother's eye.
>
> —MATTHEW 7:1–5

Ouch! I thought about the grocery store incident. I had been so busy passing judgment on the woman in the lane beside me that I'd paid no attention to my own affairs.

STUFF

The other line always moves faster.
—Murphy's Law

Jesus teaches us to examine our own intents and motives instead of passing judgment on others. Many times we find it easy to criticize others when we are wrong ourselves. A wise word of common sense I once heard says, "Sweep around your own front door before you try to sweep around mine."

Very often, the area in which we're quick to criticize others is the very area that needs work in ourselves. I need to ask myself: Have I been guilty of putting someone else down in order to lift myself up? Have I ever come to a wrong conclusion without knowing all the facts?

As Jesus pointed out, those who pass judgment on others are many times blinded by a huge plank of their own self-righteousness. In my case, when I asked God to forgive me for criticizing a woman I did not know, I had the opportunity to ask Him to help me know the difference between *judgmental criticism* and *discernment*.

Discernment shows me that there are areas in my own life where I need to ask the Lord to help me work, instead of "helping" to "fix" the lives of others.

Chapter 11

IF ANY MAN . . .

Doug and Lillian's son is a friend of mine and a fellow musician. Through him, I came to know his parents and heard their compelling story.

Doug was well into his fifties when the axe fell. At first appearance, Doug was a man of upright standing in the community. He had been married for more than thirty-five years, with two children and five grandchildren. At work one afternoon, a woman from his forgotten past entered his life by a phone call, reminding him of their one-night stand fifteen years earlier. Doug's response was his normal response—he pushed her aside.

If he thought he'd successfully staved off that first blackmail attempt, Doug was mistaken. A few days later another phone call came, this time with her alleged husband involved. They threatened to go to Doug's wife with the facts of that night. Once again Doug pushed it aside, but the threats continued to come; the amount of money they wanted grew. Doug could no longer push the threats aside; the phone calls had now become death threats on the lives of his family. Fear gripped and shattered Doug's world.

At this crisis point in Doug's life, his son was working on

an album. "If even one person gets saved through hearing your album, it will be worth all your trouble," Doug told him. He had no idea that he would be that person.

The voice from Doug's past—a past he thought was forgotten—was threatening to tear down his house of cards.

Treasure

Forgiveness is not an occasional art—it is a permanent attitude.
—Dr. Martin Luther King, Jr.

The situation in and of itself he normally could explain away, but now he was hit with the realization that there had been plenty of women since then. There was even a present one whom he had been seeing off and on for approximately twenty years. The years that Doug so easily pushed guilt and remorse aside hit him in one sudden burst. Desperate now for his life and family, Doug turned to the only One who could help him.

Doug spent hours agonizing with God. One afternoon at work—the same place where he had received the first phone call weeks earlier—Doug was finally emotionally naked. He escaped to a place where he was alone and fell to his knees, desperately crying out to God to be the Lord of his life. In total surrender Doug could now see that he believed in and feared God, but he did not love Him. As a small child he had been propelled by a stirring sermon to go forward and dedicate his life to Christ. He'd had a similar experience when he was a teenager. "Those times were nothing more than fire insurance," Doug explained. "I had no desire for Jesus to be Lord of my life."

His conversion and subsequent confession exploded like a bombshell into his family's ordinary, placid life. Not only were they dealing with one incident, but years of incidents—plus the fact that Doug's twenty-year affair was with a woman whom Lillian knew. They experienced a series of emotional shock waves, the first of which was Doug's obvious transformation. They saw a man who formerly had never cared what others thought now concerned about how his life might reflect on his Lord. The love he had never been able to feel now overflowed him, permeating his every action and decision. "Accepting Jesus is a heart-set, not a mind-set," Doug now understands.

But things weren't all that easy. While Lillian could see that her husband literally had become a new man, her own intense struggles had just begun. "Through the years of our marriage, from time to time I'd pray, 'Lord, please don't let my husband ever be unfaithful to me. I couldn't handle that,'" she said.

Now, painfully, she began to realize, "The Lord knew I had to be prepared for Doug's confession. You have to learn how weak you really are and from where your true strengths come. It would have been so easy to pack my bags and move out."

But God was about to reveal another stunning truth to Lillian. "I knew my husband had been completely transformed. Anyone could see that," she said. "But now the Lord was telling me I had to divorce myself from the *old* husband and begin again with the *new* one." Doug and Lillian then gloriously renewed their wedding vows to each other.

"When we renewed out vows, I married a new man," Lillian said. The truth of 2 Corinthians 5:17 became very visible to her as she marveled at the new Doug, so unlike the man she had known for years. But could she accept him and forgive his past? All she had ever known to be real was gone. Pictures and memories of the past were now distorted, foggy movies replaying in her mind. She was constantly wondering what was a lie and what was the truth.

The answer came through God showing her that as Doug was transformed, so was she. "We both depended on God," she told me. "Elements of forgiveness and God's grace had to be worked out in all of us." Lillian, Doug and their children grabbed on to the promise Jesus gave them—*"My grace is sufficient!"*

There have been some key signposts along the way pointing to God's amazing and continuing grace being worked out in their tumultuous situation. After Doug revealed everything to Lillian, they contacted a friend in their local sheriff's department to deal with the threatening phone calls. All fear was dispelled when they found that this couple had a history of arrests for extortion. Another astounding victory came when Lillian, without her husband's knowledge, arranged a meeting with the woman Doug had seen for twenty years—the woman whom she knew. "I forgave her. I told her she was forgiven, and that because of Christ I loved her. When I left, I felt complete peace," Lillian said.

Doug meanwhile realized that he had been saved because of the threatening phone calls. "God used a woman from way in my past to expose me—the past I thought I controlled," he said. "The woman lived in Texas, and we lived in Maine. God reached across the continent and across many years to accomplish, not blackmail, but my salvation."

Doug and Lillian have learned some awesome lessons through their experience. Lillian says she learned that she could deal with her worst fears with God's help. She says she once heard someone teach that when you're down and out and can't help yourself, you should turn and help someone else. She did that. "What a rewarding thing to do!" she told me. "It helps turn things around."

Doug learned that Jesus forgave him even before he was born. "He is creating a new life in me," he said. "Our whole family is learning to walk in new life."

Doug and Lillian will tell you their challenge has not been easy, yet the peace of God shines from their faces. Their story is one of victory, not defeat. Ask them to advise others who are dealing with adultery and possible divorce, and they offer three potent truths: God is faithful; God is forgiving; God is our friend.

"Start with forgiveness," Lillian advises. "Realize his sins are washed away. Doug truly has become a new creature. He has been washed white as snow."

STUFF

Handy stuff—
To get rid of germy
stuff on your hands,
wash them at least
15–20 seconds with
warm water and soap.

Chapter 12

〜

THE NAVIGATOR

When we buy a car, the whole family helps to pick it out. We all have to like the color; we all have to like the interior; and we all have to test drive it. It's a big family deal.

A couple of years ago we bought a car with a navigation system. This amazing computer device, once you've programmed it, tells you how to get to where you want to go. You need no written directions. Just give it the city and address and, via satellite, it tells you how to get to your destination.

For example, a lady's voice says, "In a half mile, turn right. One mile, turn left. The next half mile, enter freeway on the right." She gives you step-by-step directions. Once we deliberately took a wrong turn to see what our navigation system would do. Within seconds,

Treasure

The undevout astronomer must be mad.

—Sir William Hershel

the voice said, "Please make a U-turn immediately." Sure enough, the instructions led us right back to our driveway.

In life's journey, we believers never need to get anxious about not knowing which way to go. The Holy Spirit tells us when to stop, go or proceed with caution. I only lose my way when I fail to consult the Lord or when I carelessly stray or lag behind him. I am so glad that the Holy Spirit is our spiritual Navigator, one who leads us and guides us into all truth.

In Psalm 119:105 we learn, "Your word is a lamp to my feet and a light to my path." Through His Word, God guides us throughout our lives. Everywhere we may travel, even in unfamiliar or dangerous territory or when we make an error, He speaks in that still, small voice, our true navigation system, and tells us to make a U-turn.

God's Word instructs us about how to live, how to raise our children, how to conduct our business, how to treat our mate and so much more. Yes, the Word of God tells us when we are going the wrong way!

We don't have to worry. We may find ourselves very uncertain about which road to take in life, but the directions in God's Word even tell us which road to take in order to get to heaven.

STUFF

Stuff for your eyes— Three million Americans have glaucoma, the country's leading cause of vision loss and blindness.

Here are God's directions to heaven! Turn right, at the Light. *Then go straight.*

Chapter 13

∽

LORD, USE ME

O ur ministry hosts a music seminar each year where we invite those in our industry to lecture on various aspects of ministering through music. Young singers and songwriters always want to know how to start out. They're looking for formulas or for some A-B-C method.

I always encourage them not only to be available, but also to be usable. For example, I think of the story in the Gospels where Jesus fed 5,000 men, plus the women and children, from the contents of a little boy's lunch basket.

Even though Jesus could have fed those people some other way,

Treasure

If a man is called to be a street sweeper, he should sweep as Michelangelo painted or Beethoven composed music or Shakespeare wrote poetry. He should sweep streets so well that all the hosts of heaven and earth will pause to say, "Here lived a great street sweeper who did his job well."
—Dr. Martin Luther King, Jr.

He chose to take two small fish and five loaves of bread, bless them and feed all those people with portions to spare. The little fellow was available to Him. He didn't have much, but he offered Jesus what he had—and it was enough.

I try to remind young people that God is looking for those He can use—not just for their talents and abilities alone, but first of all, for their pliable and willing hearts.

Visiting Mama one Christmas, I proceeded to set her table with her beautiful bone china, silverware and sparkling crystal goblets. These are her best things, and they are kept in a lighted cabinet and used only on special occasions.

In her kitchen, I knew, her cupboards are filled with the sturdy, ordinary dishes we always used for everyday. Some had small nicks and chips from years of use. Glasses and mugs don't always match. In fact, some of the glasses had been peanut butter or jelly jars in a former existence, and many of the mugs are souvenirs

STUFF

If someone says something unkind about you, you must live so that no one will believe it.

from family vacations. The flatware is scratched, and a couple of knives are bent because they doubled as screwdrivers.

As I set her table, I asked myself, *Would I rather be beautiful china, sitting on a lighted shelf waiting for next Christmas, or would I rather be everyday stoneware, even if I get a few nicks or cracks or bumps along the way?*

I'd rather be used every day!

A lady was hanging a picture on her wall. When she marked the spot where she wanted to drive a nail, she realized her good new hammer rested in her toolbox outside. Rather than climb off the ladder and lose her place, she simply reached down, took off her shoe and used it to bang the nail into the wall.

The hammer was *able*, but the shoe was *available*.

So many of us have talents and gifts and look good, but we'd rather be used only on special occasions. Such big, special occasions are few and far between. God is looking for those willing to be used every day, in all kinds of situations, ready to do the job for His glory and the uplifting of His kingdom.

That's the way I want to be used.

Chapter 14

THE GAME OF LIFE

Beverly and Carl, a couple we know very well, are raising their son, Josh, in a Christian home. Lately, though, friction has developed as sixteen-year-old Josh attempts to be "cool" like the other kids. His parents hate Josh's baggy pants, earrings and ear-splitting music. Since Josh believes he needs these things to survive, tension often reigns—especially between father and son.

Whenever Carl and Josh are at each other's throats, Bev steps in to keep the peace. Whenever her mother's instinct takes over, however, Carl says, "Don't treat him like a baby."

Bev thinks her husband's approach is usually too heavy-handed. So the household stays in a continual tug of war centered around Josh's rebellion. Mom and dad pull the reins, Josh pushes the buttons and the boundaries, and there's friction in the home. No one seems to be on the same page as another.

There's one thing, however, that Josh and dad still have in common. They both love an old-fashioned game of checkers. Carl, a natural strategist, plays to win. Josh is more like his dad than he'd like to admit—he also plays to win.

Father and son love to banter and compete over checkers, and Bev loves to watch them.

"You know, the game of checkers is a lot like the game of life," Beverly observed. Josh bent lower over the checkerboard, frowning and obviously tuning his mother out. How many times had he heard his parents preach the same old generational sermon? How his parents' grandparents found themselves in disgrace if they were caught smoking in the boys' room. How his parents' parents might have been expelled from school for sneaking a beer. And, in their own generation, Carl and Bev told him, rebellious kids had begun to use marijuana and LSD.

Treasure

Any relationship is like a house with an upstairs—it has two stories.
—Dolly Parton

But now, in Josh's generation, as they frequently reminded him, the enemy has intensified his activities to the point that his weapons against our young people actually kill them. Josh's generation is desperately addicted to drugs, alcohol, tobacco and sex. They die of overdoses. AIDS is proliferating.

"Yes," Bev goes on, almost to herself, "the devil hates Josh's generation." But Josh, like any other teenager, is tired of hearing lectures from his parents.

"Checkers is like the game of life," Bev repeats. "As long as you stay on your side, in the safety zone, you are safe. You are secure. But the moment you leave your side of the board and go out into the middle, you jeopardize your safety. You risk tangling with your opponent."

Josh immediately moved toward the center of the board.

"You're moving out," his mom observed. "You're choosing a secular college and a different set of friends. You know," Bev worried, "once you've crossed that center line, it's almost impossible to get back to safety."

"That's right," his dad said, absently. He frowned, concentrating on the board. "It's difficult to come back, unless you have a king."

Bev says she sat straight up, startled. Carl wasn't talking philosophically or spiritually, she knew. He was talking *checkers*. But she rejoiced. "You can't come back unless you have a King," she emphasized.

You cannot escape the bonds of sin unless you have a King. "The wages of sin is death, but the gift of God is eternal life in Christ Jesus our Lord" (Rom. 6:23).

It's best to stay in the safety zone, as Beverly told Josh. Stay with the Lord. But as she reflected, even if you do cross the center line in life, you *can* come back—if you have a King.

STUFF

Children and grandparents are natural allies.

Chapter 15

~

PLUGGED IN

We never think much about electric power—we just expect it to be there. But one very busy day at our office, the electricity cut off.

Our ministry's staff workers include my husband and me, one full-time assistant, two part-time helpers and dozens of volunteers. We're a busy operation, not a huge one. The day the power failed, however, we were all scurrying like ants, attempting to prepare for several events across the country.

Treasure

Shoot for the moon, and even if you miss, you will fall among the stars.
—Norman Vincent
  Peale

We were thinking logistics and details, not power.

Then our office went dark. Nothing worked. No computer, no telephone, no fax, no music-on-hold—nothing. We rushed to the windows and looked out. The major highway on which our office building is located was swarming with workmen widening the street. Obviously they had caused the problem, and our entire office building had lost power.

We were helpless. We could do nothing without electricity. To make things worse, this was Friday, a very hectic Friday. Needless to say, we could only pray and wait to be reconnected to our energy source so we could resume our daily work.

That episode made me stop and think. I had time to thank God that I was "hooked up" to the power that connects us to Jesus— the power of the Holy Spirit. He guides us and leads us into all truth. He gives us wisdom, comfort and power to withstand the enemy.

STUFF

Before you try to shine, be sure you are hooked up to the power source.

But when we are not connected to Jesus through the power of the Holy Spirit, we are defenseless. We're left sitting in the dark, helpless, unable to accomplish the purpose God has ordained us to do.

I once saw a bumper sticker that read:

> No Jesus, no power.
> Know Jesus, know power!

Without Jesus, we have no hope. We have no source. We lack the strength and the power we need to overcome the evil of this world. We have no power to become victorious. We cannot become an overcomer.

But when we know Jesus as our Lord and Savior, we are connected to Him—heart to heart. We can become overcomers through Jesus Christ who loves us. We must stay plugged in, connected to the power we need. Our unfailing source of power is Jesus, who is the Light of the world.

Chapter 16

Chapter 16

EATING MY WORDS

If you're married, you know the difference a word, spoken or unspoken, can make. There's plenty in the Bible that tells us we should be careful with words. In Proverbs, for example: "A word fitly spoken is like apples of gold in settings of silver" (Prov. 25:11).

By the seventh year of our marriage, the honeymoon period was over. Charles and I, like many other couples, had learned to bicker and to find fault with each other constantly. Sure, the love was still there, but often our words didn't match up with it. Each could find plenty to criticize about the other. We began to antagonize one another a lot—and we did it with words.

We could have periods of peace and even discuss why we weren't getting along. Then Charles would say something hurtful or insensitive to me, and I'd use my extensive vocabulary to belittle him.

The more I talked, however, the less he said. And the less he said, the more I talked. Then we'd go back on the warpath.

This unproductive behavior went on for years. Still, as angry as we were at times, we were determined to make our marriage work. By the grace of God we kept on keeping on. But we still remained largely unaware of the huge impact our words, for better or worse, had on our happiness.

I don't know when the healing began, but I know that through much prayer, God gave me the grace to accept my husband exactly as he is—and God gave Charles the grace to accept me. More and more, we see that each of us is an asset and a complement to the other. Our personality differences are many, but our marriage has become stronger because of them. The fact that we are opposites has proven to be our strength.

Treasure

The only people with whom you should try to get even are those who have helped you.
—Mae Maloo

Charles meets life head-on, seeing most issues in black and white. I always have to weigh the different shades of things. Charles weighs an issue with his head; I weigh it with my heart. Now we can consider an issue from both standpoints and together work out the best way to handle things.

Like most women, however, I always enjoy words of appreciation. Once, when someone referred to me as a "Christian star," I felt a little uneasy at the term, but took it as a compliment. After the concert, my no-nonsense husband reminded me there was only one "Star"—and they killed Him!

According to behavioral experts, women are the "sayers"

and men are "doers." Because we women are so verbal, it's easy to talk rings around the good man we love, forcing his verbal skills to dry up even more! And if he mispronounces words, as Charles sometimes does, and we continually correct him, no wonder some of us feel starved for sweet talk from our man. Others actually leave the strong, silent type for some glib talker who'll lead them down the wrong path in life.

Heaven only knows how many words from my husband's mouth had to be corrected by this schoolteacher wife before God corrected me for my own mispronunciation—for my own good. What's more, He corrected me publicly, at the height of a successful concert, just prior to my closing song one evening.

The concert had been a blessing. God's presence was truly evident. As I began to introduce my final song, I started to praise Him. "Jesus is worthy of all our glory!"

The people responded with excitement, "Amen! Amen!"

"Jesus is worthy of all the glory, He is worthy of all the adoration, all the adulation, and all the *ovulation*!" The moment I said it, I heard my mistake. Of course I meant to say *ovation*, but in my attempt to use alliteration, my syllables got ahead of me, and I misused the word.

STUFF

If you want to do something positive for your kids, work on your marriage.

To make matters worse, I tried to apologize and correct my mistake. The audience was very forgiving. The concert, in spite of me, ended on a high note, and God was glorified.

God used that incident to humble me and allow me to see that I too am capable of mispronouncing a word now and then. I well remember my discomfort, and the sting of being "corrected." That night I learned that I don't need to correct others, but rather to watch my own words, each one of them, seeking to make—not perfection—but love, tenderness, kindness, healing and encouragement my goal.

Verbal women, unite. Let's put some words of love and praise out there in our hurting and abusive world!

Chapter 17

MR. GOOD DEAL

I asked Sandy Smith, an Atlanta teacher, speaker and minister's wife, to tell this thought-provoking story in her own words.

Nestled in the softly rolling hills of Tennessee is a small town that time has not altered. It was dark when we reached the city limits, and signs of Christmas were everywhere. Each of the old-fashioned light posts lining Main Street bore a huge twinkling snowflake, and every house seemed lit and decorated like something from the past.

Christmas was in the air, but as we drove slowly through the streets I found myself wondering about what might be hiding behind the Christmas lights. What pain? What need?

The catfish house looked inviting. Although it was only seven o'clock, the evening rush hour had come and gone. Our fresh-faced waitress seemed far too young to be wearing the wedding ring on her finger. With a wide smile and bright eyes, she asked, "Hi! Can I git y'all somethin' to drink?"

We perused the worn menu. Everything looked

good! Soon hand-dipped onion rings, hush puppies, fried okra and catfish filets arrived, all smelling sumptuous. We groaned as we filled our stomachs way past full, listening as townsfolk at nearby tables talked of the weather, horses and catfish.

A different world. A whole new world, I marveled.

It was well past eight when we headed down Main Street to the brightly lit town square. First Methodist Church stood on our right, but First National Bank, aged, stalwart and impressive, ruled the square, which otherwise was surrounded by small businesses probably passed down from father to son to grandson.

Treasure

If God be your partner, make your plans larger.

—D.L. Moody

Thornton's Men's Store had gone out of business. City Jewelers had not. The dress shop and furniture store probably looked much the same as they had for years.

But one store on the square stood in dramatic contrast to the others. Its windows were filled with plastic Santas, toy trucks and dolls wearing slightly soiled dresses. The sign across the door read MR. GOOD DEAL. Painted on the window was the message, EVERYTHING FOR SALE CHEAP—EXCEPT HORSES.

Mr. Good Deal himself ushered us into the store.

"Come on in!" he bellowed. "Buddy," he shouted to a young employee, "see this man here? He's rich as can be! Hundred dollar bills stuffed in all his pockets!"

My husband laughed. "I'm a preacher, sir. You know what preachers make!"

We wandered through the store, stepping over rotten places in the floor. The place was enormous, and the abundant "stuff" that filled it was making its way even up the creaky stairway. We saw rows and rows of musty-smelling clothes, dingy toys and a rack of Christmas cards, yellow with age, that must have sat on some drugstore shelf for years.

The odors of long-stored, forgotten items assaulted us. Mr. Good Deal himself smelled of hard work and sweat, and he looked as disheveled as the goods he sold. I wondered who bought stuff here and what kind of customers he served.

Eager to escape the dust and mingled odors,

STUFF

According to Good Housekeeping, *food buffets are not your friend. Chances are, you'll keep eating long after your hunger has disappeared.*

we soon began making our way through the maze. We felt hemmed in by the disorderly piles of aging merchandise. But Mr. Good Deal was following us, speaking to the fact that my husband is a preacher. "Sometimes I don't know 'bout church folks," he stated. "A homeless man came through here last year 'bout this time, and there wasn't a person or a church in this town that would buy him a meal!

"I took him home with me for a few days."

I found myself turning and looking this plump, per-spiring old fellow in the face. My feelings were beginning to change. What kindness he had shown to someone whom the "religious folks" in town had no time or thought to help!

Mr. Good Deal followed us to the door. "If you got any kids needs Christmas, bring 'em to my party at the barn next week," he invited. "Last year I gave clothes and toys to eighteen hundred needy kids! Folks bring 'em over, and we take care of 'em!"

I turned and looked again at this amazing man. Somehow I didn't see his scruffiness nor did I smell his sweat. I saw a man who showed the character of Christ far more than I—or many other Christians—do. We had come to this town to share the gospel, but this man was living the gospel—in the same common, unadorned sur-roundings Christ knows so well.

This rusty little man probably never goes to church, I thought. *Even so, he is the Good Samaritan. He is doing what Jesus would be doing in these hills at Christmas time!*

I had judged this man. I also had judged the "church people" of this town, and now the spirit of a Holy God was tapping me on the shoulder. "What about you?"

Early Monday morning we drove out of town, heading back to Atlanta and home. Soon they'd unlock the doors of the First Methodist Church. The bank would hum with business, and shoppers would enter the dress shop and furniture store. But Mr. Good Deal and his enormous store, bulging with outdated merchandise, stayed in my mind.

I thought about the lip service so many Christians give, and I thought about this humble, unpretentious man who, like Jesus Christ, opens his heart to the little children and to the unwanted and homeless stranger in town.

God, help me not to forget this village where I heard from You, through the loud voice of a simple man, not too good to be real.

Section II

~

GOD'S PROMISES

As we seek to find the hidden treasures of God on our journey through life, we find that we will not know all the answers. That's when we learn that God is faithful, always true to His promises. Though we cannot trace His hand, we can always trust His heart. We can take God at His Word, for He is the ...

Response to every request.

Chapter 18

THE GIFT OF GRACE

He sat in the seat near the aisle, reading his book. I sat at the window reading mine. I drank my soda and was careful not to disturb him. After years of flying on airplanes I have learned not to intrude into other people's space. He was a middle-aged man with graying temples, casually dressed, sipping a mixed drink. He was the first to break the ice. He introduced himself and asked what I did for a living.

"I'm a singer and songwriter," I said. I have learned after years of meeting people on airplanes not to blurt out, "I'm a *gospel singer*." It makes people nervous. Once I sat next to a fellow traveler who was enjoying his second Bloody Mary when he asked that question. When I replied, "I'm a gospel singer," he immediately put down his drink. When the flight attendant asked if he would like another, he shook his head and ordered a glass of milk. I don't like making people nervous. I want to be a light, but I don't want to blind anyone with it. For the moment I would seek to understand and wait for the right moment to be understood.

So I inquired about my seatmate's occupation. He owned a small restaurant in a little town in the North Georgia

Mountains. He described his home, nestled in the foothills, where he could see the beauty of three states from his front porch. His restaurant opened only on weekends to accommodate tourists who visited the nearby historic town or the state park located in the area.

He seemed to enjoy his bustling business and the people it attracted. He remarked that

Treasure

Real servants teach us more by what they do than by what they say.

since his restaurant opened only on weekends, he had decided not to accept credit cards. It wasn't worth the hassle—or the percentage it cost to accommodate them. So he accepted only cash and personal checks at his restaurant. He smiled as he continued telling his story.

During weekend business, he often encountered vacationing families who had exhausted their cash reserves by week's end. Assuming they could pay with a credit card, some enjoyed their meals only to discover later that credit cards were not accepted. This brought on immediate panic for unprepared guests who had visions of washing dishes or peeling potatoes in the kitchen until closing time. Each time this happened, a waiter would promptly usher my seatmate, the restaurant's owner, to the table.

My seatmate had a generous way of resolving the sticky situation. He would first reassure his guests, and then he would present them with his business card and ask them to mail a check to cover their bill upon their return home. His guests would be delightfully surprised and relieved, for this kind of service is unheard of.

This very kind gentleman and restaurant owner told me that in the years since he began the no-credit-card policy, only once had a guest's bill gone unpaid. He remarked that he often receives card and letters of gratitude from people who have been recipients of his generosity. A number of people have left the restaurant as a guest with an unpaid debt, and later returned as a friend. Many have brought others to the restaurant to meet this man with such a kind and liberal heart.

As our plane came in for a landing, I thanked my seatmate for telling me his story and wished him well in his business. I shared with him that what he did in his small restaurant, God did for the whole world. I told him that his generosity is a gift—the gift of grace.

That is exactly what God does for us. He gives to us before we have a chance to earn it or ask for it. We owe Him a debt we could never pay. He paid a debt He did not owe. The Bible says, "While we were still sinners, Christ died for us" (Rom. 5:8). Almighty, righteous, holy, merciful God stooped down and offered poor, wretched, dark, sinful earth a gift. It is a gift that we do not

STUFF

One in six Americans has a fear of flying.

deserve and can never earn. It is the gift of grace through God's Son, Jesus Christ.

We deserve to pay for our sins with our lives. Romans 6:23 says, "For the wages of sin is death..." But wait. Here's the good news. "...but the gift of God is eternal life in Christ Jesus our Lord."

Credit-card companies may extend a twenty-five-day grace period, but God's grace extends all the way into eternity. The late Donald Barnhouse, a noted Bible scholar and pastor, perhaps said it best: "Love that goes upward is worship; love that goes outward is affection; love that stoops downward is grace."[1]

---

[1] Charles Swindall, *The Grace Awakening* (Nashville, TN: Word Books, 1996).

Chapter 19

UNFAMILIAR TERRITORY

It was chilly outside, and the windows were steamy with condensation, but our house was warm and filled with wonderful aromas on the inside. The pinto beans and ham had been simmering all afternoon and were cooked to perfection. The mixed greens salad was freshly tossed. All I had left to prepare was the crowning glory of my Southern meal—the cornbread. But when I went to the cupboard to gather ingredients for the cornbread, I discovered that there was no cooking oil!

Now I don't know about you, but in our house pinto beans and ham *must* be eaten with cornbread. It's an absolute necessity. So I scurried to the neighborhood grocery store, plunging straight into the aisle of baking supplies where I knew I'd find cooking oil. My eyes quickly scanned the shelves as I searched for my favorite brand.

Intent on my mission, at first I hardly felt something—or someone—touching my knee tentatively. As a mother of two, I intuitively knew the grasp was nonthreatening, and the tugging continued as I browsed the shelves. At last I looked down into the face of a precious toddler, probably about eighteen months old. Eyes round as quarters as they scanned my face, he realized he was clinging to the wrong pants leg, and he bolted as fast as his toddling feet could carry him.

I found the oil, and as I reached the end of the aisle I turned for one last glance at my little intruder. There he stood, his arm now clinging to a much slimmer, longer, leaner leg. The other arm led to a thumb, nestled content-edly in his little mouth. At that moment, he looked up to catch me admiring him from afar. He cracked a bashful smile that totally melted this stranger's heart. I waved ridiculously, as most adults do when trying to entertain a baby, then turned to take my place in the checkout line.

Treasure

Opportunity knocks only once. Temptation rings the doorbell.

That encounter taught me a thing or two. I believe the moment that little one grabbed my leg, he knew immediately that it was not the one he'd toddled around before. It didn't take him long to think things through, probably rational-izing, *If it feels unfamiliar, looks unfamiliar and moves in an unfamiliar way, it's probably not safe—and I'd better head for familiar territory.*

Have you ever ventured down an unfamiliar path, and heard the still, small voice of God whispering to you to turn around—but you continued to linger? Have you ever flirted with strange desires? Deep in your heart, you knew it wasn't right, but you held on anyway, struggling to get comfortable.

Has your mind ever toyed with foreign thoughts, giving in to fleshly desires? Your heart tried to warn you, but to no avail? An old adage says, "Opportunity knocks only once. Temptation rings the doorbell."

The Bible strongly warns us against giving in to temptation. Temptations are everywhere, but God's power in us enables us to resist:

> No temptation has overtaken you except such as is common to man; but God is faithful, who will not allow you to be tempted beyond what you are able, but with the temptation will also make the way of escape, that you may be able to bear it.
>
> —1 CORINTHIANS 10:13

When we fall into temptation, we should pray and ask God's forgiveness, and He will forgive. Ask Him to strengthen you with His power to resist the evil one, and He will. I don't know what you may be struggling with, but I do know that God is greater than any temptation. People who struggle with temptation can always come to Jesus.

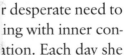

STUFF
You should never say no to a gift from a child.

r desperate need to ing with inner con- tion. Each day she

·ut of, and then into, a relationship
                                        ·vas not married. But then she had a
                                        with the Lord Jesus Christ. Jesus
                                        ier life that caused her to look for
                                        ·s.

Jesus knows exactly how it feels to be faced with temptation. Jesus was tempted by Satan, yet never sinned (Matt. 4). Jesus is ready, willing and able to empower us in every battle against temptation.

The next time you venture into unfamiliar territory, turn and run home to Jesus. Temptations are inevitable. If Jesus was tempted, we certainly will be tempted also. Inevitably you will find yourself in a situation that doesn't look like Jesus, doesn't feel like Jesus and doesn't sound like Jesus. And no doubt, you will hear the still, small voice of God speaking to you, telling you to resist. When you hear that voice, remember that the name of the Lord is a strong tower. The righteous run into it, and they are safe (Prov. 18:10). We find Him a powerful source of strength in our times of weakness.

Chapter 20

LIKE A BIRD

The gymnasium filled with people, but we were arriving for a worship service—not a sporting event. Gathering for one of a series of evening services, hundreds of people were streaming in, eager to hear about the God who sets captives free. Some would hear that message for the first time.

Wonderful hymn singing began the evening. A man told of being introduced to Jesus that very day when local church members visited his home. The choir sang, then I stood to give my vocal solo. It was only after I returned to my seat in the bleachers and the evangelist began his sermon that I saw them—two tiny sparrows darting among the top row of bleachers, high in the rafters near a row of windows.

I wondered if anyone else noticed. Dwarfed by the huge gymnasium, the tiny prisoners desperately sought a way out. Fluttering their wings, they flew against the windows time after time. Attuned to the birds' obvious fear and frustrations, I soon felt too distracted to hear the evangelist's words. My thoughts took over: *Surprising to see birds inside a building . . . birds should fly free . . . outdoors is their territory, trees their home and windy breezes their front yard.*

Birds are not meant to be trapped....

Most likely, the windows had been opened during gym class that day, I mused. Maybe the birds flew in to escape the hot sun, or perhaps they'd found a new place to play. Then, at day's end, someone shut the windows, trapping the sparrows inside. How long had they flown from space to space, endlessly seeking a way out? I felt so sorry for them.

Treasure

*Earth has no sorrow
that heaven
cannot heal.*

After the service, perhaps I could find a janitor willing to climb high into the bleachers and open the windows, I thought. We'd all cheer when they flew free!

Then I realized that no janitor would be on duty that late, and my heart sank. I prayed that tomorrow the gym teacher, the janitor, a student—*somebody*—would climb up there, open a window and make freedom possible.

I'd missed a lot of the sermon, but now I heard the speaker ask that we bow our heads for prayer. He invited those enslaved by the chains of sin to come forward and receive Jesus Christ—their key to freedom.

Then the parallel bore in on me, hard. Each of us, like those tiny, helpless sparrows, can so easily get trapped in a cruel, indifferent world, held hostage and hoping, begging, for release. Unable to free ourselves, we roam helplessly, aimlessly, trying to find a way out.

We try to pacify our emptiness with busyness, afraid that if we cease running about, we'll have to face the reality of our misery. When we are silent, our pain screams too loudly to allow us to rest. We try to dull that pain with drugs, alcohol or addictive relationships. We continually bump our heads against what looks like the answer. We hope for an open window, only to recover from our stupor as banged and bruised as if we'd just emerged from the house of mirrors at the county fair.

We ask ourselves questions: *How did I get myself into this mess? Whatever happened to living "free as a bird"? When will life stop playing cruel jokes on me? How did I get into this wild, senseless madness?*

Our world desperately needs someone to come along, open the windows and doors of our cages and set us free. God sent freedom to us in the person of Jesus—the Way, the Truth and the Life.

I'd like to think that some kind person saw those pitiful birds and released them from their prison in the gym.

STUFF

The greater the struggle, the greater the stuff.
—*Bishop T. D. Jakes*

I can imagine that at first sight of the open window, the birds took off on wings of freedom and never looked back. I can hear them singing melodies they never had sung before.

Just as simply, Christ sets us free. Our world is held hostage, trapped by sin. There is only one Savior who can open our cages and release us. His name is Jesus.

I have tasted that freedom for myself. I know what it's like to be trapped, with no way out. I have tasted bitter tears of frustration as I looked for the keys to my deliverance in people, places and things. I have sung the ballads that called for others to love me, validate me and comfort me. Too often, others only betrayed me. I learned firsthand that to lose one's freedom is to embrace death. To gain freedom is to gain life.

Jesus Christ, for my sake and yours, conquered everything that entraps us—sin, death, hell and the grave—and released us from the prison of sin.

It feels so good to be free. No more chains. No more cages. No more traps. Maybe you've been seeking a way out of your own prison. Perhaps you've looked to others for your answers, only to realize they are bound by their own chains. Like a desert mirage, one dead-end relationship after another leaves you burned out, hungry and thirsty for satisfaction and life. But earth has no sorrow that heaven cannot heal. In the middle of our desert stands Jesus, the Oasis. He stands with arms wide open, beckoning you to come to the water of life.

Jesus understands your situation. He is familiar with your pain. He knows how it feels to be bound. He was nailed to a cross and executed for crimes He did not commit to pay ransom for you and me. Held prisoner in a tomb for three days, He arose victorious, conquering anything and everything that threatens our freedom.

Jesus holds the keys to your deliverance. If you want freedom, ask Jesus *now* to break the chains of sin that bind you. Ask Him to help you. He will.

When Christ sets you free, that settles the issue for all time. No need to seek another person, place or thing. Just ask Jesus. "Therefore if the Son makes you free, you shall be free indeed" (John 8:36).

Chapter 21

NEVER SAY NEVER

When I looked in the mirror recently I saw an all-too-familiar face. That smooth brown skin, the almond-shaped eyes, the trademark widow's peak that has been in our family for generations, the smile you can see in a hundred family photographs...

But it wasn't *my* face I saw in the mirror—it was *my mother's. It's amazing,* I thought, *that the older I get, the more I seem to look, sound and act like my mother.* That's wonderful, though, because she is the most beautiful and sophisticated mother on the face of God's earth.

When I was younger, sporting a miniskirt and shiny knee-high boots, Mom seemed ridiculously old-fashioned. I told myself I'd never dress like her or wear my hair that way. She pushed her hair up. She wore shoes with pointed toes. She told my sister, brothers and me, "Eat your beans. They're good for you." "Save your money for a rainy day." Or, "Someday you'll thank me for this." Then there's the warning I still don't understand: "Be sure you wear clean underwear. You never know when an accident might happen."

Mom cooked things like pinto beans and ham and corn-bread. She and Dad seasoned their food with hot sauce.

Often there was a bowl of boiled okra on the table. If there were three foods I absolutely disdained as a kid, they were pinto beans, things seasoned with hot sauce and the crusty part of cornbread. My sister and I always fought for the soft middle piece.

But as the old folks say, "Never, never say never."

Decades later I am married with children, doing my best to train up children (and sometimes my husband) in the way they should go. And my tastes, meanwhile, have changed. I'm too old now for miniskirts and patent leather boots. I've learned there's nothing tastier on a rainy Monday than a good bowl of pinto beans and ham. To top it off, add a couple of dashes of hot sauce and give me the corner piece of cornbread with nice, crusty edges. Is that heaven or what?

Also, like my mother, I appreciate beans as an excellent fiber source. A big pot will last several days, and beans are very economical. Thanks, Mom.

For years my mother wore her hair pushed up so it resembled what some call "big hair." She had beautiful natural curls and waves. As a teenager, I thought curls and waves were fine for Mom, but not for me. I was proud to sport my neatly shaped Afro!

But times change. Recently I began wearing my hair straight again, page-boy style, which looked great except for the left side, which seemed a little flat. But when I pushed my hair up a bit, a funny thing happened. A wave naturally fell into place. It looks rather nice.

I was about sixteen when platform shoes came out the first time. Mom's pointed-toe, high-heeled shoes looked so uncool next to my hot pink suede platforms. Mom said that high heels make you look long and lean. She wore lots of black, pointing out that black always is fashionable, classy and makes you look thin. Those days I wore black only to funerals when I was singing in the choir—with my hot pink suede platform shoes, of course.

Treasure

This is all the inheritance I give to my dear family: The religion of Christ will give them one which will make them rich indeed.
—Patrick Henry

But after having two children, eating late meals after concert performances and developing a love affair with nacho chips and guacamole, I opt for anything that makes me look tall and thin, long and lean. Any woman knows that a nice black dress or suit always makes a nice fashion statement, but of course the look would not be complete without dressy black high-heeled shoes.

Just as tastes in food and fashion change over the years, our spiritual aspirations also change. *I'll never be a missionary,* I thought in my youth. The only missionaries I knew were older, White, single, celibate women who went to places like Zambia, lived with the natives and never came home.

Since I didn't fit that description, I thought I was off the hook. I was younger, Black and married, with children. I felt certain I'd never become anything like a missionary.

However, God has a way of changing our minds, even about that. I've come to realize that I'm either a missionary or a mission project. Traveling throughout the United States and most of the continents, spreading the Good News of the gospel of Christ in song, is the greatest mission I have ever been assigned.

I'm neither White nor single, and I have two very fine sons. I know too that many others are far more qualified than I, but when it comes to sharing the gospel, it only requires us to love God and His people enough to desire to see their hearts changed and their eyes opened to the love of Jesus Christ. I find that so very easy to do.

I have found the Good News is even better than we know. Living for Christ and sharing His love—becoming a *missionary*—affords us undreamed-of privileges and adventures. If God guides me to an open door, I know He will provide whatever I need to walk through it.

Whatever our mission, learning to trust God, allowing Him to teach us new truths, journeying into unknown places and following Him wherever He leads—probably things we never dreamed of as kids—is the best place we can possibly be.

Sometimes it might seem like jumping into the deep end of the pool without knowing how to float. But God will become my Lifeguard, or He will teach me how to swim. How many times my mother's old-fashioned faith showed me that!

STUFF

Did you know—
There are three billion
women who don't
look like supermodels,
and only eight who do?

Without those cool knee-high boots or my hot pink platform shoes, today my heart desires to discover the deeper truths of God and walk with Him, like my mother, shod in classic black high-heeled shoes, toward a place of spiritual maturity.

Maturity? Now, that's funny. I never thought I'd use that word.

Chapter 22

THE LETTER

Her name is Yolanda, but her friends call her "Yo-Yo." Now thirty-one and the mother of three, her story is all too typical—first a normal life, marriage, babies—then an introduction to the agony of drugs.

When Yolanda talked with me about her struggles, she spoke of her despair at finding a way out of her bondage:

> All I lived for was the drug. I'd go to sleep high, and do it all over the next day. I started to lose my possessions, my car and then my job. The rent didn't get paid, and my kids weren't getting cared for properly. I lost all self-respect and the respect of my family and friends. Finally, I hit bottom. I went to jail.

Yolanda's release from jail did not coincide with her release from drugs, however. She soon slid back into her old habits. At last, desperate for help, she telephoned a home for women and checked herself in. "That's when I found my missing piece," she says. "The missing piece was God. That's where I began my relationship with Him."

Yolanda's story has a glorious outcome. When Yolanda finally began her journey to wholeness by checking into a place where she could find help, she wrote the following eloquent letter, addressed to "Mr. H." (heroin).

Dear Mr. H.

Today is no ordinary day. I know it's been a while since I dealt with you, but I feel I need to express myself to you. You and I had a strong relationship. Though we had our ups and downs, we never let anything or anyone come between us. You picked me up when I wasn't feeling well. You seemed always to be around in time of need.

Treasure

No God, no power.
Know God,
know power!

I have to say, you really changed my life! I'm actually getting chills as I write to you. These chills are happy chills, not sick chills. (I had to clear that up so you'll get the correct understanding.)

Looking at how I feel today, Mr. H., I was a sick woman to call those "happy times." I recall you telling me everything would be all right, that I could go on hurting my family and loved ones because you'd be there to back me up! I should have known you'd fail me sooner or later. I should have picked up on you earlier, but I was blind!

Enough is enough! I need to tell you that I realize what you did to me. There's no need for me to use harsh words, because I'm not living that way today. I'm trying to make a change in my life, and I don't need your help. It's time for you to move on and stay out of my life. "Friends?" I hear you asking me. No, never! I wouldn't want to be, or want to meet anyone else of your kind. I must have been blind to think we could live a happy life together. What was I thinking? I've got to hand it to you...you had me hooked!

Some relationships end and you can remain friends, but ours can't be that way. You need to know that today I am a strong Christian, walking my Christian walk with my Father, and getting higher and higher every day. Get it right, though, Mr. H.—I'm high on Jesus. Once again I need to explain the word "high" to you. I know where your mind is.

See, I'm working on Yolanda today and the goals I want to achieve in life. I am building a firm foundation, and I am standing on it. Instead of calling on you, I call on Jesus, because I know He will never leave me, and He won't tell me any-thing wrong. Thank You, Jesus!

STUFF

The write stuff— Keeping a journal may help you gain more of an understanding of what makes you ner-vous, happy or sad.

I recall you telling me there's no life out there for me, and you were all I needed in this world. Well guess what, my ex. I've got life today. I'm a newborn

Christian, learning more and more about my friend, Jesus. My sweet Jesus! I am living for God, and my God is a jealous God. He doesn't like it when someone of your background tries to pull one of His kids away from Him. What I'm saying is, I've got *life* today, and I'm going to live it to the fullest.

I'm going to sign off now. You're not worth my pen and paper. Please don't try to look me up. And don't worry, I'm not going to come looking for you. In my eyes, you no longer exist.

Just Me

Perhaps you know someone who needs to read Yolanda's brave words, written to her enemy. Jesus said, "The thief does not come except to steal, and to kill, and to destroy. I have come that they may have life, and that they may have it more abundantly" (John 10:10).

Do you know a Yolanda? Perhaps your own child, or someone in your neighborhood? These days life-stealing addictions permeate our society. They kill, steal and destroy. Some say we'll never win the war on drugs.

Meanwhile, thousands of others like Yolanda have discovered the way out. *Jesus* is the Way, the Truth and the Life. He can and will restore His own. He never fails.

If each one would reach out for Jesus Christ, we could rid our nation of the scourge of drugs. Yolanda represents someone in your family, your neighborhood, your school, your workplace or even your church. Ask God to show you how to help lead a desperate, addicted person to Jesus Christ for redemption, healing and a gift of new life.

Thank You, Jesus, for Yolanda and for the thousands of

others like her whom You have saved. May God give us His same compassion toward each of His hurting and despairing ones. May we never turn our backs on Yolanda. Jesus never will.

Chapter 23

I REMEMBER WHEN ...

I don't now what it is about the phrase, "I remember when..." It brings a feeling of comfort to think back to simpler times. There's something consoling about recalling bygone days. Though I'm not as old as some who rock on their front porches on balmy evenings and reminisce, life did seem simpler even when I was growing up.

Treasure

We must adjust to changing times and still hold to unchanging principles.
—Jimmy Carter, Inaugural Address, January 20, 1977, quoting his high school teacher Julia Coleman

During the few decades I have occupied the planet a lot of things have changed.

I remember when a gas station was called a "service station." My father would drive across a long black hose that caused a bell to ring, and the attendant hurried to wait on us. "Fill 'er up," Dad would say, and while the uniformed man pumped our gas, he also checked the oil, the tire pressure and washed the windshield—all with a thank-you and a smile.

I remember the drive-in theater. Profanity and nudity were not seen or heard at the movies or on television. Black-and-white television signed off at midnight with a devotional and "The Star-Spangled Banner."

I remember when we prayed in school and hymns were sung at every school assembly. Teachers maintained control of their classrooms. The Ten Commandments hung in the school's front office. Each grade performed a Christmas play, complete with a nativity scene. We said, "Merry Christmas" and "Happy Easter" instead of "Happy winter holidays" and "Have a nice spring break."

I remember when we listened to major league baseball on the radio at night. We looked forward to our Sunday school picnic. A man's word was his bond. The customer was always right. Parents disciplined their children.

I remember when we dressed up to go shopping, dressed up to fly on an airplane and dressed up to go to church.

I remember when *bad* meant bad. *Cool* meant chilly. *High* meant above one's head. *Marriage* meant forever. *Rap* meant to knock. *Sue* was a girl's name. *Gay* meant happy. Nothing

STUFF

Twenty years ago, models weighed 8 percent less than the average woman. Today, models weigh 23 percent less than the average woman.

came out of the closet except a coat, hat and an occasional vacuum cleaner. To *surf* meant to glide on a flotation device on top of the ocean. The *net* was something you used to catch fish.

I remember when the computer was somewhere in a big warehouse in the Midwest. The only satellite we'd heard of was "Sputnik."

I remember when *pot* was something you cooked in. *Weed* was an unwanted plant. *Ice* kept your drink cold. *Speed* meant driving your car too fast. *Crack* was a hole in the floor, and *Coke* was a soft drink.

Today the only thing certain is change. Change means letting go of the comfortable and familiar. That's why we don't like it. And have you ever wondered why it's so difficult to change someone else—and even more difficult to change one's self?

Change is a fact of life. Politicians change their policies. Fashion designers change hem lines. Methods and modes of communication advance. The housewife (oh, this is an opportunity to be politically correct), or houseparent, will find quicker ways to cook the evening meal.

But unlike our ever-changing world, Jesus has always been, is always being and will always be the same. Remember Hebrews 13:8: "Jesus Christ is the same yesterday, today, and forever."

Amen.

Chapter 24

∽

TREASURED MEMORIES

Our family shares a rich spiritual heritage with five generations of preachers and pastors in our lineage. It is an honor to be included among those men and women who have loved and feared God for generations. And as you can imagine, whenever we get together, it's fascinating to hear the family stories. Some are new. Some we've heard again and again, but we still laugh or cry at the same places.

These gatherings always end up around the table over one of Mom's famous desserts. Soon after the water is heated for tea and the cake is out, our stories begin. "I remember when . . . " brings back cherished thoughts of some family members and introduces younger ones to memories of others long passed on.

I'll never forget hearing about my grandfather's death, for instance. Though barely able to read or write, he was known as a great preacher. For years, he pastored in the Delta of Mississippi, visiting each of the four churches he served one Sunday a month.

When in his early eighties and the visiting preacher for a nearby church on a fifth Sunday afternoon, they say my grandfather preached his sermon, sat down in the stately wooden chair in the pulpit and simply went home to be with Jesus. What a precious memory.

My own parents served their first and only church for nearly forty years. I can honestly say I not only heard my father preach and teach from God's Word every Sunday—and plenty of Wednesdays—but I saw it lived out on a daily basis. Around our house it was commonplace for Bible stories or principles to find their way into everyday conversations and activities.

Treasure

Maybe you have a heritage of faith that includes men and women who have served the Lord for generations. Or maybe that heritage of faith begins with you.

One example of this happened when I was small and our family went to Canada for our summer vacation. We all love to fish, so we could hardly wait to get to the lake. We arrived at our campsite by midafternoon, with everyone excited to pitch in and help set up before evening.

My father and Uncle Joe struck out to find a grocery store where they could buy food, bait and other supplies. When they had not returned by dusk, however, we began to get concerned. It was well past dark by the time our menfolk got back to our camper. Dad immediately launched into the story.

En route to the store, Dad and Uncle Joe had enjoyed viewing the Canadian landscape, the sparkling lake and the glorious scenery. They were especially intrigued to discover an Indian burial ground that contained the remains of Indian chiefs and an adjoining museum filled with tribal artifacts.

Soon they found a store, did their shopping, then headed back to our campsite. It didn't take long, however, for them to realize that nothing along the roadside looked familiar. They stopped at a small gas station to ask directions.

The station owner asked Dad and Uncle Joe for the name of the campsite where we were staying. Neither could remember it. "What road is it on?" the man asked. They didn't remember that either. "What direction is it in?" By now, all three had begun to realize that our men were truly lost.

Then the gas station owner, concerned and wanting to help, asked the key question: "Do you remember any signs or landmarks you saw along the way?"

Dad's face lit up as he recounted the event. "I remembered the valley of the dry bones," he told us. "I told him our campsite is near some dry bones!"

The gas station owner recognized Dad's description of the Indian burial ground and museum, so it was easy for him to point them in the right direction. Dad's reference to Ezekiel 37 was not just an Old Testament story, but was as familiar to him as if it were in today's newspaper—and

STUFF

Stuff on z-z-z's— The National Sleep Foundation says that 65 percent of American adults don't get enough sleep.

a very welcome road map when they needed it most. Deuteronomy 6:6–9 says:

> And these words which I command you today shall be in your heart. You shall teach them diligently to your children, and shall talk of them when you sit in your house, when you walk by the way, when you lie down, and when you rise up. You shall bind them as a sign on your hand, and they shall be as frontlets between your eyes. You shall write them on the doorposts of your house and on your gates.

The Bible commands us to incorporate its principles into our daily living. Maybe you have a heritage of faith that includes men and women who have served the Lord for generations. Or maybe that heritage begins with you.

Start today to share your passion for the Lord with those you love. You'll find the Word of God serves as a trustworthy landmark along the journey, even when life seems confusing and unfamiliar.

It's the only signpost and the only lamp we'll ever need to lead us safely home. It's our most dependable, accurate and unfailing guide . . . especially when we are truly lost.

Chapter 25

❧

ALL RISE

From the moment I set foot in Mrs. Melvin's first grade class, I knew I wanted to be a schoolteacher. I've always loved the sound of clicking chalk on the green slateboard as the teacher wrote out the day's lesson. The long, shiny linoleum halls that led from the playground to the classroom always heightened my anticipation about what we might learn next. And it always was a big deal to go down to the janitor's closet and clean the erasers by holding them over a huge vacuum-cleaner machine.

I still smile at the thought of creating a masterful Mother's Day greeting card from construction paper, glitter and Elmer's glue. The ultimate treat, however, came when Mrs. Melvin asked me to entertain my classmates by singing and playing the old upright piano while she ran a quick errand to the office.

School was a success for me. Good teachers, good grades and good friends made it a fun place to be. So there was a natural progression from Babbie the student who sat behind a small desk in the middle of the row to Mrs. Mason the teacher who stood in front of a classroom.

I taught in middle school for seven years and truly enjoyed

it. But then I began to get calls to sing at small gatherings, at a Bible study or a ladies' meeting. Little by little, my singing schedule began to conflict with my teaching job. By now we had a son in elementary school and a brand-new arrival, which added to the balancing act.

Treasure

God works best when your back is against the wall.

Needless to say, this young wife, mother, teacher, piano instructor and singer grew more exhausted each day. In 1984, after much prayer, I quit my teaching job so I could launch a full-time music ministry. Charles was struggling to maintain a small business. I had given up a regular paycheck, retirement and health benefits. God, however, had given us both the certainty that this was His plan.

That summer I learned of a music seminar to be held in the Rocky Mountains, which offered all kinds of classes taught by music industry professionals, nightly concerts and competitions with record company executives as adjudicators. Pictures in the brochure showed beautiful mountain settings and featured quotes from some of the industry's most renowned artists who endorsed the seminar.

This sounded like a good idea, and we considered going. I had done a little songwriting and had made a few public performances, so I figured I qualified. We had no money for airline tickets, so when a Shell gas credit card arrived in the mail, we believed this good idea had turned into a GOD idea. By now Charles and I had everything planned: We would charge our gasoline and use our little cash for accommodations and food.

In early August, filled with anticipation, we headed west in my husband's truck, driving all day and well into the night before we stopped at an inexpensive motel. The next day, however, we ran into a big problem. There were no Shell gas stations west of St. Louis! By the time we reached the conference center, high in the Rocky Mountains, we had spent nearly all our money.

Charles and I pinched pennies by eating bologna sandwiches and peanut butter crackers in the tiny cottage we had rented for the week. Each day we attended sessions that taught us about music ministry, mission opportunities and the craft of songwriting. A new world opened up before us.

For the first time I learned that songwriting is not just inspiration, but also quite a bit of perspiration. A great song has a strong title, a rhyme scheme, a memorable chorus and a universal theme. In other words, someone besides your mother has to like it.

The songwriting judges were brutally honest. "This is OK," they said about the song I entered, "not really bad, but not really good, either. The words are a bit trite. The melody is a little stale and a bit too familiar." I took the critique personally. They might as well have been talking about one of my children. "Babbie, we love you, but your baby is ugly."

Maybe I would do better in the vocal competition, I thought. On the last day of the conference, having made it to the vocal finals, I was to compete with three other singers.

The mountain air by now had taken its toll on me. The climate gave new meaning to the phrase "high and dry." The lack of humidity had made me hoarse, and by now I was suffering from an eye condition that had flared up. I had to compete with a patch over my left eye.

By competition's end, I held in my hand a third-place trophy. Since several hundred participants had competed that week, a third-place trophy actually was quite an accomplishment. However, I felt deeply disappointed—not because I thought I should have come in first, but because I was displeased at my own performance.

I was troubled by the circumstances I had encountered during the week. I felt I didn't make the grade. I felt average. I felt like the best of the worst, and the worst of the best. All I had to show for the money we spent, the distance we drove and the disappointments we suffered was a third-place trophy.

For days after that, I replayed the week in my head. What if I had sung another song... or entered another song I'd written into the competition? Why had I competed in the first place? Why did my eye have to flare up so I had to sing before all those people with a huge piece of gauze over my eye?

The enemy's voice went around and around in my head. "You are a no-good songwriter and a third-place singer. You're only good at mediocrity. You'll never amount to anything in the music business."

But I know this much is true: The enemy is a liar and the father of lies. I prayed and asked God to help me rely on what I knew, not what I felt. I knew God had a purpose for my quitting my job. I believed in my heart that He would not bring me this far only to leave me. I began to fight my fears with the ammunition of the Word of God.

One day about three weeks after the conference, I was walking through my home when the thought occurred to me that one day we will see Jesus face to face, and earthly performance will no longer matter. If we have claimed Jesus Christ as Lord, a third-place trophy will be of no significance. Earthly accomplishments will pale in

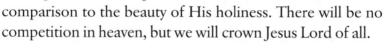

STUFF

God makes a miracle of the mess of your life.

comparison to the beauty of His holiness. There will be no competition in heaven, but we will crown Jesus Lord of all.

In my mind's eye, I saw a courtroom crowded with people. The bailiff announced, "All rise; all rise. The honorable Judge is presiding over the courtroom."

There appeared Jesus Christ, the Judge, the Advocate, the Jury and the Faithful Witness. I realized then that we will not rise to our feet when our names are called or bask in standing ovations from the crowd, but we will stand before our Supreme Judge, the Head Adjudicator, the Author and Finisher of our faith—and offer *Him* our unending ovations of praise! I penned these words:

> All rise. All rise
> To stand before the throne
> In the presence of the Holy One.

All rise. All rise
As we worship the Messiah.
All rise![1]

That year I sang *All Rise* in my concerts, and I experienced the presence of God in many worship services as never before. Opportunities to minister began to come from various denominations and organizations across the nation. God used that song to launch my music ministry. As Charles often says, I really didn't quit teaching; my classroom just got bigger.

I often think back on the summer of 1984 and that first experience at the music conference. It amazes me to see how God turned what I saw as devastating defeat into His catalyst for victory. Once again He showed me He is faithful to restore whatever the enemy has stolen.

Right now, you may be walking through a valley of disappointment. You may feel as if you have given your all, only to walk away empty-handed. You have gone the extra mile, only to arrive at your destination to find the journey was in vain.

Praise God! This is the perfect time for God to show up and show off in your behalf. This is a grand opportunity for God to take what seems like a curse and turn it into a life-changing blessing.

God works best when your back is against the wall and you have depleted all your resources. When you have given your all, God steps in to administer healing for the hurts. He is the God who makes a miracle of the mess.

By the way, there is a divine addendum to this story.

I returned to the Rocky Mountain music conference the following year and again entered the songwriting and vocal competitions. God allowed me to win first place in both categories.

All Rise was the Grand Prize-winning song at that 1985 conference. Scott Wesley Brown, one of the songwriting competition judges, recorded my song a couple of years later. By 1987, it would gain the title of most-recorded inspirational song of the year.

---

[1] "All Rise" by Babbie Mason. Copyright © 1985 by C. A. Music (a div. of C. A. Records, Inc.). All rights reserved. Used by permission.

Chapter 26

THIS IS A TEST . . . ONLY A TEST

Sometimes I feel troubled by the way we Christians respond to challenges. As Jesus reminded us in John 16:33, "In this world you will have tribulation; but be of good cheer, I have overcome the world."

If we know we'll face trials, why are we not more prepared when they happen?

We have been given every vehicle, tool and device we could possibly need in order to become overcomers. We have the Holy Bible in every conceivable version. We have Christian books, Christian music tapes, Christian television and Christian radio.

We also have Christian preachers, revivals, conferences and prayer groups . . . yet some of us seem weaker today than ever before.

It's frustrating also to realize that as many Christian marriages are in trouble today as those in any other segment of the population. And you'll find just as many Christians as secular clients in therapists' offices for counseling.

With all we have at our disposal, why do so many Christians seem weaker and more fragile than ever before? When I pondered that question, the Lord showed me one day that in reality, any "bad" circumstances I come up against are, as the Bible says, a test of my faith. A test...only a test.

I remember, in the days of black-and-white television, when programs sometimes were interrupted for special announcements. A voice said, "This is a test. This is only a test." And when difficult times arise in my life, that statement sometimes flashes through my mind: "This is a test. This is only a test."

In 1 Corinthians 10:13, the Bible tells us, "No temptation has overtaken you except such as is common to man; but God is faithful, who will not allow you to be tempted beyond what you are able, but with the temptation will also make the way of escape, that you may be able to bear it."

Why, then, don't more Christians believe that truth? As a teacher, I never quizzed or tested my students on anything I had not taught them. If they had a problem, I knew they had been prepared to find the solution.

In my own life that also holds true. When problems arise, God has taught me beforehand how to overcome them. He has given each of us the answer needed to figure out our own way of escape.

Think back to your student days. Take the slothful student who always procrastinates. He puts off studying, watches TV and goes out with the guys. Exam week comes, but he doesn't begin working until the night before his test. He stays up late, using the crash-studying technique, but due to sleep loss, that technique is not effective. By the time he starts taking his exam, he feels tired to the point of exhaustion, yet he knows he has not covered the material. No wonder he's nervous about the test, and he begins it with anxiety and fear.

When the student looks at his test paper, he feels unsure of his materials and can't remember his acronyms or formulas. He guesses at some of his answers. By the time his test grade arrives, he is not surprised to learn he didn't do so well.

Treasure

God's people have found that the most precious fruit often grows in the midst of overwhelming difficulties. Faith grows best on cloudy days.
—Jim Cymbala,
Brooklyn Tabernacle

The good student, of course, is the kind God is looking for. This student applies himself to his work, methodically and consistently. He applies what he learns to his life and to his heart, "precept upon precept, line upon line," storing and using this knowledge to his great benefit.

The night before the exam, this student reviews his work, then gets a good night's sleep. If he finds a difficult problem on his test the next day—or even three or four—he has time to think them through. He knows he possesses the ammunition he needs to solve those problems, because he has studied throughout the semester. The good student feels confident that he did well. Sure enough, when his test is returned, he has received a great grade.

It's the same in our lives as believers. If we don't study God's Word, we can predict what eventually will happen when our test arrives. We may attempt a "crash course," anxiously seeking the right principle or scripture to help solve our problem, but we know we are standing on an uncertain foundation because we did not study God's Word earlier and learn how to apply it to our heart and life.

The good student in life consistently studies, doing as the Bible instructs: "Your word I have hidden in my heart, that I might not sin against You" (Ps. 119:11). When we do that, building our lives line upon line and precept upon precept, we may be confident that we can pass those tests.

No, life isn't fair. In the classroom, you study the lesson, then you take the test. But in the classroom of life, you take the test first—then study the lesson. Perhaps you are going through some tough circumstance right now that will encourage you to become a good student of God's Word and better apply His princi-

STUFF

Three reasons for entering the teaching profession: June, July, August.

ples to your life. More likely than not, something in your life—your house, car, children, health, job or finances—has come under attack. It is the Word of God, its study and its application, that will help you overcome such everyday challenges.

Remember, this is a test. This is only a test.

He already has provided a way of escape for you.

Chapter 27

~

RUNNING THE RACE

Ann Chastain, one of my former middle school pupils, grew up to run an impressive number of marathon races: the Boston Marathon, the Peachtree Road Race, the Alaska Marathon, the New York Marathon and others.

Ann, now a lovely, accomplished young adult, was someone I wanted to interview on *Babbie's House*, my Christian television program. On my show, live before the world, Ann challenged me to enter the upcoming Atlanta 10K Classic race always held on Labor Day morning.

Reluctantly I said *yes*. Now I love to walk, but have never raced—especially uphill! This race covers 6.2 miles. It is known as the most difficult 10K because of its steep hills. In fact, it's mostly all uphill along one of Atlanta's main thoroughfares.

I began to train with Ann. *How like the Lord*, I thought, *to have someone I once taught now become my mentor, example and teacher.* I found myself rising at the crack of "dark-thirty" each morning, walking one mile, then two, then three, then four—with steep inclines on our training course.

The first time we trekked up such a steep hill, I noticed that the in-shape runners took it as if it were nothing. But I, who had never seen such steep grades (even though this one was just a mile from our house!), found every step painfully difficult. My legs ached, my feet hurt and I wanted to quit.

Philippians 4:13 says, "I can do all things through Christ who strengthens me." I took that verse as fact, and determined to make it to the top of the hill. Midway I stopped, breathless and hurting, and quoted that scripture aloud. This famous ten-finger prayer literally got me up the hill. With my hands at my sides, I'd count on my fingers, "I...can...do... all...things...through...Christ...who...strengthens... me." And I would get to the top of the hill.

"Let's walk down, then back up one more time," Ann would say. It was brutal training, some of the most intense I'd ever put my body through. Early on, I realized just how much this nonathlete, Babbie Mason, was out of shape. But I also realized, as the apostle Paul wrote in 2 Corinthians 12:9, "My [God's] grace is sufficient for you."

As Paul continues, "Therefore most gladly I will rather boast in my infirmities, that the power of Christ may rest upon me. Therefore I take pleasure in infirmities, in reproaches, in needs, in persecutions, in distresses, for Christ's sake. For when I am weak, then I am strong" (vv. 9–10).

I began to see the correlation between running that course and the Christian walk, where sometimes the hills are so steep spiritually that we cannot attain them by ourselves. We have to cry out to God for help and hear Him say, "My grace is sufficient for you."

The week of the race, I walked 6.2 miles through my

neighborhood. I had never walked that far in my life. This was one of the greatest moments of satisfaction I'd ever known. I had placed this body under subjection. I had said to this body, "You have climbed this mountain. There will be others to scale, but with God's help, nothing will be too hard."

Treasure

Aim at heaven, and you will get earth "thrown in"; aim at earth, and you will get neither.
—C. S. Lewis

This reminded me of Paul's words in 1 Corinthians 9:24–27:

Do you not know that those who run in a race all run, but one receives the prize? Run in such a way that you may obtain it. And everyone who competes for the prize is temperate in all things. Now they do it to obtain a perishable crown, but we for an imperishable crown. Therefore I run thus: not with uncertainty. Thus I fight: not as one who beats the air. But I discipline my body and bring it into subjection, lest, when I have preached to others, I myself should become disqualified.

As I compared this physical race to my Christian, spiritual race, I clearly saw I needed to become more disciplined. I felt compelled to challenge myself, spiritually *and* physically. There was a sense of urgency to step up my fervor for the Lord, to increase my strength training as well as my faith training.

The night before the race I felt too hyped up to sleep. I tossed and turned and prayed until 3:30 in the morning. Then I got up and drank some herbal tea. Even with two hours of sleep I felt refreshed. I had to arise at 5:30 to get an early start prior to the race. My biggest challenge, my greatest competition, I saw, would be racing against *this body and this mind.*

On Atlanta's famous Highway 41, going north, that first hill of our course loomed impossibly steep. I was told, "Pace yourself through that hill, and you can make it." By the time I reached the top of that difficult climb, I was rejoicing in the Lord. Soon I was to discover that at each mile marker a big band was stationed, playing music that would keep me pumped full of encouragement.

Looking around, I saw fellow runners who found this effort painful to endure, but we all kept going. A young man in a wheelchair had to go it alone, yet so many others around him were calling out words of encouragement, rallying him on. When he made it to the top of that steep hill they cheered for him. I'm not sure he could have reached it without the others who rooted for him.

STUFF

I didn't fail ten thousand times. I successfully eliminated, ten thousand times, materials and combinations that wouldn't work.
—*Thomas Edison*

A middle-aged lady near me obviously had little training, but she had entered the race because her husband and his new girlfriend were in it. She was quite discouraged, and I was trying to inspire her to keep going. About that time I looked up and saw a billboard sign that read, "You don't have to go through this alone." I nearly jumped out of my shoes.

"Look at that billboard!"

The woman began to weep, and she continued on. Amazingly, my encouraging her encouraged me.

Nearing the end, I spotted another former pupil of mine, now in her twenties, standing among the spectators with her two small children and her mother. They were there to encourage and congratulate me! Such caring, interest and genuine well-wishing touched something deep in my heart.

And then I was nearing the finish line. The greatest band of all sent powerful music toward us, urging us on toward triumph. *This has to be something like heaven,* I thought. The people along the way, applauding and spurring us on, reminded me of that great crowd of witnesses we read about in Hebrews 12.

I crossed the finish line. My coach was there to bestow upon me my prize—a medal and a T-shirt. I got something very personal that morning—a new vision of a God who goes the distance with me and every other struggler. He is always exhorting and infusing us with courage, never leaving our side. He stays with us until we complete our course. He urges us not to quit. And at the finish line, He greets us with joyous music, applause, prizes and praise.

The 6.2-mile race up Highway 41, Atlanta, taught me again an age-old truth: "I can do all things through Christ who strengthens me" (Phil. 4:13).

Chapter 28

LIVING SATISFIED AND SINGLE

My good friend Donna I. Douglas (not *The Beverly Hillbillies'* Donna Douglas) and I have written songs together for seventeen years and have spent a lot of time together, but there's one thing I'd never asked her: "Why have you never married?"

This woman is "Auntie Donna" to my boys, has taken care of them for me at times and fits in like a member of the family. So much so, in fact, that when Chaz was twelve, he was astonished to learn that we are not actually related—which is funny since Donna is very blond, fair-skinned and green-eyed. (Just goes to show my son is color blind!)

But there's another thing I didn't know about Donna. Why is she, at midlife and still single, so unusually happy and well-adjusted? What makes her different from some single women I know who obsess about their marriage prospects and can hardly ever talk about anything else?

I knew Donna has plenty of men in her life. Yet she never married and doesn't seem to feel left out. What is the story? When I dared to bring the subject up to her, she candidly answered my questions.

"When I was college age, and then later in my twenties, I

and everybody else expected me to be married with a houseful of children," she said. "But I never found the person I wanted to be with 24/7. Then and now, my friends and career fill my life. I have great, close men friends. We have great conversations and great companionship. I enjoy dinners, movies and the beach with the guys. And as for children, I am 'Auntie Donna' to the world."

Would she like to be married? "Sure," she said. "But I also think singleness, for some, might be a calling. So many women are so restless about the marriage issue. My singleness—up to this moment, anyway—has been a calling. And even if marriage never happens, my life is already meaningful."

Treasure

You matter to God at every age and at every stage of your life.

I thought about all Donna packs into her days: author, speaker, songwriter, screenplay writer—not to mention, I thought, the way she speeds to the rescue when anyone needs her. "As they say, if you're not happy single, you won't be happy married," she went on, reading my mind. "We need to be whole, happy and content. When two half-people come together, it does not make a whole marriage.

"Even in my desert experience," she continued, "I never saw marriage as the answer. Whenever I struggled with something, the Lord was always faithful to send friends. Once I was crying and praying about a job decision I'd made when the phone rang. I didn't answer, but when I checked my answering machine later, it was you, Babbie, reminding me of 2 Chronicles 20:15: 'The battle is not yours, but God's.'

"Another time when I was praying and praising, the Lord said 'Jacob's ladder.' I looked it up. Part of the passage reads, 'Everything your foot touches will be yours, and your descendants shall be as many as the dust.'" (See Genesis 28:12–15.)

I'm not married, Lord. I won't have any descendants.

"And God spoke to my heart, 'Everything I create in you that is birthed from your pen becomes your descendant.'

"God answers when I call on Him. What singleness has done for me is to allow God to become everything to me. I have such intimate times with Him. That's what the wonderful gift of being single has meant to me. As Paul writes in 1 Corinthians, it can be a blessing."

But what about children? "When I need children, I call yours or others for trips to the museum or painting or swimming with dolphins," she reminded me. "In Isaiah 54 God tells me that I will have more children than the married wife, and that the Lord will be my husband. When I read that, it was like a great big hug!

"Because I am single, I've been able to have three pregnant teenagers in my home. I have nurtured abused children. I've had the privilege of imparting God's goodness and pouring His love into some scared and neglected children. I'm a great hugger, and I can encourage. I would absolutely die for some of my kids. I have the love without the labor pains."

So what does Donna think a woman should do if, with all her heart, she desires marriage?

"Women should rest," she emphasized. "If there's any

issue that possesses us, we have a spiritual problem. Unless we lay it on the altar and learn to rest in God, it will not change. If you place your energies on hunting a husband, chances are your relationship to the Lord needs to be improved." Donna believes women need to ask God to make us comfortable with ourselves, just as we are. "Only when things are right with Him, and we are complete in that relationship, are we ready to move into the next relationship," she explains.

"If marriage is in God's plan for your life, and you are seeking His best, you don't have to worry. You don't have to fret, be anxious, put on your hunting gear or search the streets.

"You can know that if God can paint sunsets, fling the stars into space, turn water into wine, part the Red Sea and conquer death forever, He can bring the spouse you need into your life—*in His time*. We can rest in that, just as we can trust Him in every other issue in our life."

Here are some terrific ways Donna Douglas encourages women to live *single and satisfied*.

- Put God first in your life. Get to know Him. The love He pours into you will be the love you'll extend to the person He sends into your life.

- Learn to love as God loves. Wait for Him to provide that perfect person He knows will fulfill your life.

- Should marriage not be God's plan for you, you will have learned from Him how to be satisfied. His plan is that we be satisfied in all things. That can only happen if we first fall in love with Jesus.

- Certain areas of relationships are not to be indulged in, so guard yourself against erotic movies, books and other things that bring temptation in these areas.

Donna reiterates, "What we don't feed will die. I stay away from anything that might entice me to go there. You have to make an effort to guard your mind and heart. Otherwise you'll have many struggles you are not meant to have."

Does this advice work? Take one look at dynamic Donna, one of the most creative and fully actualized women I know, and you'll be convinced that she is single and satisfied. And if you are single, you can be satisfied, too.

I'm glad I asked.

STUFF

If you pursue happiness, it will elude you. But if you focus on your family, the needs of others, your work, meeting new people and doing the best you can, happiness will find you.

Chapter 29

LOST AND FOUND

Thousands of women today are searching for their lost children—runaways, kidnap victims or babies they once gave up for adoption. Ruth Wade knows all about that kind of grief. She lost her two-year-old daughter for twenty years. Not only has God miraculously reunited them, but He gloriously healed the sorrows and hurts accumulated during those long, sad years.

Ruth's story begins during her teen years. One of six children born to hard-working, loving and strict parents, she enjoyed an exceptionally happy childhood. Her father was strong, strict and loving. He provided well for their family. Ruth's mother stayed home to rear her children, and her father sent them to parochial schools and instructed them in their Roman Catholic faith.

"Daddy was strict about curfews. We had lots of rules and regulations, both at school and at home. We children knew the lines we couldn't cross," Ruth told me. But before she turned sixteen, she fell in love and crossed one of those lines. When her sweetheart finally persuaded her to have sex, she surrendered—just one time. Ruth soon discovered she was pregnant.

"I knew what this would do to my parents," she said. "I was too scared to tell them. Instead, my teenage boyfriend broke the news—and then he turned his back on me."

As she had expected, Ruth's parents were heartbroken. They decided to place her in a home for unwed mothers where she would deliver her infant, then give it up for adoption. "You have disappointed me greatly," her father told her. "I don't even want to see you in this condition."

Ruth moved into an unwed mother's home in another town. She had never before been away from home, and she arrived sick and miserable. It didn't seem to matter that she was the only Black girl there, however, since the other girls seemed equally mixed up, unhappy and afraid.

One day Ruth woke up so sick that the staff sent out for medicine. When it arrived, she was shocked to find her father standing at the door. Wordlessly, he handed her the medicine.

"How are you?" he asked.

"I'm doing OK."

Despite her surprise, Ruth noticed that her father no longer seemed angry or judgmental. She saw concern and compassion on his face. "His eyes told me he forgave me, but he didn't say the words," she said.

After she took the package he had brought her, her father immediately left. Two days later, the strong and apparently healthy man suffered a heart attack and died in his sleep.

Ruth learned of her father's death two days after he died when her mother came to relate the stunning news. "You must be strong," she said, then relayed the facts. Ruth collapsed in grief. "I was convinced I killed my father," she told me tearfully. The depression that set in lasted throughout her confinement. When her baby arrived, Ruth was still anguishing.

But she kept the baby. Returning home with her son, she attempted to resume a normal life, despite some horrible emotional impediments. Even the sight of her beautiful infant at times brought waves of guilt and remorse flooding over her.

Treasure

You can't change the past, but you can ruin the present by worrying about the future.

Ruth became pregnant a second time when her son was eighteen months old. Once again it had happened the first time she and the young man had a sexual encounter. The eighteen-year-old, filled with ideas about a strict and sometimes vengeful God, felt sure He must be punishing her for her sins.

"This time I could not tell my mother," she said. "I was afraid I'd kill her, too. She didn't deserve to have my second disgrace on her shoulders."

The teenager found a job and an apartment and, with her toddler, moved away from her family. She lived like a hermit. Only a cousin and two trusted friends knew her situation. This pregnancy was difficult also, especially since she had no money for prenatal care.

"I arranged for a childless friend and her husband to take my baby and raise it," Ruth said. "I believed the child needed two parents. Trying to raise my son alone taught me how hard single parenthood can be."

The girl's second birthing experience proved terrifying. Labor pains hit with such ferocity that she had to crawl to a neighbor's apartment for help. The concerned neighbor took Ruth's little boy and called an ambulance, but the situation became increasingly nightmarish once she arrived at the hospital's emergency room. Ruth remembers both ambulance and hospital staff members yelling at her because she had no money and refused to give them any personal information. Meanwhile, she thought she was about to die of fear and pain.

Days later, the ecstatic surrogate parents arrived to claim Ruth's newborn daughter, and the exhausted new mother again began attempting to put her life back together. For two years, she says, she saw her daughter often. But when she wanted her little girl returned to her, her friends moved and changed their names. She found it impossible to trace them.

This began a pattern of cat-and-mouse moves that continued for twenty years. No matter how hard she tried, a despairing Ruth could never locate her child, nor could she turn to others for help. She kept her anguish to herself.

Did she pray? "Of course," she told me. "The nuns taught me to reverence Jesus, and they taught us the Ten Commandments, too. But I knew I'd broken one of those commandments, and when I prayed to Jesus and begged for His help, I never felt I deserved it."

Then came marriage, happiness and another baby girl. One month after the baby's birth, however, Ruth's husband was killed in an accident. By now she had moved to Georgia, away from her home in Detroit. An Atlanta friend invited her to attend a Christian weekend retreat led by Kay Arthur. When Ruth invited Jesus into her heart and asked Him to become Lord of her life that weekend, she set the miracle wheels into motion.

"This changed me," she said. "I was still weeping for my dad and my lost daughter, but now I had begun to feel peace for the first time in my adult life. Hope began to take root in my heart."

Like many other women, Ruth needed deep release from years of emotional turmoil. "God showed me that even more than guilt feelings, I was dealing with years of hidden pain and grief," she explained. "He made me realize, too, how amazing it was that He had allowed me to see my daddy one last time that day when he brought medicine to me. God allowed me to see the compassion on my daddy's face and to know he still loved me. I thank God for showing me that."

Ruth continued to grow in the Word and to strengthen her spirit, but nothing seemed to quench the feelings of longing she felt for her daughter. She never stopped trying to track down the surrogate parents, though all attempts led to dead ends. She and her sister, Patricia, called a couple of organizations that claimed to find missing people. No one even returned their calls. Ruth and Patricia decided to give the situation entirely to God. They began to pray and believe according to Matthew 18:19, which says, "If two of you agree on earth concerning anything that they ask, it will be done for them by My Father in heaven." They stood totally on the Word of God and let it go.

Within a matter of two weeks the answer came. Ruth by

now was remarried to a publisher who took her with him to a professional conference in Detroit. At this event she met a man she had known years earlier, who was able to tell her how to find the woman who had her daughter.

"She had changed jobs and moved repeatedly," Ruth explained. "But when I found her, she agreed to have my daughter (Athena) call me. The baby I had left with her was now a young married woman with children—and I wondered if she'd even want to talk to me!"

God arranged a glorious reunion. Not only did Ruth's daughter gladly accept her, but she resembled Ruth more than any of her other children. Emotionally, it was as if they had known each other forever. From that point forward, the two have had regular telephone calls and visits, and both rejoice in the Lord.

STUFF

Stuff for Mom—Motherhood is not for weaklings. After all, it started with labor.

"My daughter is a strong Christian, and we share Jesus with one another," Ruth said. "Soon after we met, we attended an evening church service where people were giving testimonies. My daughter stood and give her testimony. She said one thing I'll never forget. She said, 'I am so glad my mother did not abort me.'

"I'll never be able to tell you what those words meant to me," Ruth said, weeping.

Almighty God, who redeems even some of our worst

mistakes and decisions, once again proved His mercy and grace. His ways are awesome!

I asked Ruth what she would say to another teenager like herself, or a bereft mother in her situation. "Do not abort your baby," she pleaded. "Give your baby up for adoption, believing God will place him or her in the perfect home. Or ask God for grace to help you raise your child.

"Remember, God is a God of reconciliation. He can do what no man or woman can do. After twenty years of searching, I still could not find my daughter—but God could find her, and He did.

"Trust in God. Never give up hope. In His time, He can reunite and reconcile. And He can heal each one concerned."

Chapter 30

SET FREE

My brother Alan says his rebellious spirit developed very early. The second of our parents' children, outstanding in sports from grammar school on and raised in a happy family that applauded his many victories, Al nevertheless believed he was growing up in a very restrictive lifestyle.

"Church several times a week was a requirement, and my personality conflicted with that," he told me. "I wanted to do the things other guys did—go out when I wanted to, come in late, drink if I wanted..."

Al's boyhood dream was to become a professional baseball pitcher. Every sign pointed to his attaining that goal. He passionately pursued sports in the form of neighborhood sandlot football or softball games, then discovered basketball and decided he'd become the next Wilt Chamberlain.

He had unusual success, always. In high school he became the first freshman ever to make the varsity baseball team, and he led the team in hitting. As a senior, he had begun to attract some notice. And when he enrolled in Western Michigan University, some told him he was making a mistake. The school was too rigid, they said, and would not let a Black man join the team.

In Al's case, however, they were wrong. He became the first Black pitcher in the school's history. In one exciting game he shut out America's number-two college team. However, he soon came to believe his coach was as difficult as he'd been warned he would be. Their constant tiffs and arguments, which Alan believed were racially motivated, kept him on the bench. It seemed an unhappy and unacceptable situation for a rising talent. But things got even worse.

Treasure

Sow a thought and you reap an action; sow an action and you reap a habit; sow a habit and you reap a character; sow a character and you reap a destiny.
—Samuel Smiles

That summer as my brother pitched in a local baseball game, he heard something snap in his pitching arm. At that instant he realized his future career had vanished. Despondency and hopelessness set in. Soon Alan turned to serious gambling. It gave him the same high as an intense ball game always had. Always strongly competitive, he discovered hustling turned him on, as did his experiments with marijuana.

"Of course, there's no future in gambling," Al explained. "You're not going to win. But by now I had suffered an attitude shift. I knew I wasn't going to win, that my dreams were busted." Despite knowing the odds of winning at gambling were something like one thousand to one, he persisted, eventually robbing and stealing to support his addiction.

"Gambling gets your adrenaline flowing," he explained.

"It becomes a devastating addiction. For me, the only thing that could break that addiction was the worst addiction of all—crack cocaine. I know heroin addicts who try every way in the world to beat that addiction; changing to crack cocaine is the only foolproof way to beat it. Little by little I saw my life weaving itself into a web of addiction."

Breaking the law became routine. The first time Alan appeared before a judge, however, God gave him space to repent. His lawyer, who knew him from college, persuaded the judge that despite the seriousness of the charge, Al's excellent past character and his respected family background should be taken into consideration. The judge pronounced an extremely lenient sentence. But the young man, by now thoroughly under the influence of drugs and gambling, returned to his old ways.

So it went for years. Alan entered into several forms of reckless and dangerous behavior, which predictably led to jail and prison. Each time he'd embark on a three-day drug binge beforehand, knowing he'd have to endure cold-turkey withdrawal during his incarceration.

What was he thinking? "That someday I'd straighten myself out," he told me. "Someday later, I'd give this stuff up and live the life our parents raised me to live. *But not yet.* I'd keep the crack and the easy money I made dealing drugs, and the gold chains and fast company, a while longer."

However, some stunning events made Al's timetable soon come to a climax. One day his "best friend," crazed by drugs and convinced that Alan had stolen from him, produced a Lugar pistol and shot him in both legs. When Al fell, the man placed the gun to his forehead to finish the job. My brother heard a click, and his assailant pocketed the weapon and went into his house, leaving the wounded man sprawled out on an ice-crusted sidewalk.

Bleeding and struggling to stay conscious, Al watched minutes later as his friend, the man's wife and her mother each stepped over his body to get to their car and drive away. For forty-five minutes the helpless man lay bleeding, wondering if help would come in time.

But God again saved Alan Wade. Our aunt, it happened, was driving her son to the dentist to treat a sudden toothache, when for no reason she took a wrong turn off the freeway. Attempting to correct the mistake, she drove past my brother, and our cousin spotted Al lying on the pavement. Laughing, he got out of the car, thinking Al had slipped and fallen on the ice. Then he saw the blood.

Despite three days in the hospital and eight slugs removed from his legs, Alan soon was once more on his way to prison. As he returned, hobbling on crutches, the irony struck him. This was the facility where our father had preached and ministered to inmates for nearly forty years. How often he had warned his son that his rebellious ways could lead him to this place!

During an earlier incarceration Al had attended a prison prayer meeting where he accepted Christ. Once released, however, he immediately returned to his old habits. "I acknowledged Jesus then, but did not allow Him to become Lord of my life," Alan confessed. "I was still very much in charge of my life, for better or worse."

This time, however, things had to change. How much longer could he evade death? He described the experience of entering prison. "My first day there was as profound as the day I got shot," he recalled. "You sit in a bull pen, stark naked. They spray you with insecticide, search you for contraband, then you dress in prison blues.

"You get a tuberculosis shot, an identification card, a number, a bedroll, toothpaste, soap, pen and pencil. Then the electric door opens and you walk through. You see hundreds of 'bird cages' stacked six tiers high. One of these belongs to you. All eyes are on you as you walk in. The noise is unbelievable.

"My legs were in terrible shape, and my gallery was four flights up. As I climbed those stairs I heard someone call my name, then another, and another—all former buddies."

What changed Alan? "I had finally hit bottom," he said. "My pastor brother visited me. By now I was feverishly thinking about whom I could persuade to get me out on bail. Realistically, I knew bond would be denied because of my bad record, but I couldn't stay in that cell. I spent every waking moment figuring how I could get Mama or somebody to help me.

"My brother said, 'Instead of worrying about bail, you'd better worry about your salvation.' He was right. I thought of all the ways I'd tried to manipulate my family, my friends and even God. I knew it was time for me to surrender."

Alan had a twenty-month-old son at the time. He had told his girlfriend that upon his release he would marry her and relocate his family; they would attempt to build a real life. He wanted his son to have the advantages our parents gave us. But could he change? And did she believe him? Would she wait for him to complete a two-to-six-year sentence?

For the first time, Alan intended not only to kick his serious drug addiction cold turkey, but to turn away from his entire corrupt lifestyle. The challenge seemed formidable. Slowly he was beginning to realize that the lifestyle he had chosen for himself proved far, far more restrictive than the one our parents chose for us.

"I had years of prison time ahead of me," he said, "and there was absolutely nowhere I could go except to God and His Word. My circumstances seemed hopeless, but God is faithful. Old hometown friends visited me in prison, and we worshiped together. I began to get back into the hope game.

"Because of my son I was determined to steer myself back to God. I had made it perfectly clear to my girlfriend, now my wife, that this time I would not return from prison as the same man who entered it. The hardest part was when she and our son visited. When they left, I'd have a pain in the pit of my stomach. He was growing so fast. He had begun to talk, and he'd beg Dad to come home with him.

"I began placing my trust in God. I had to trust Him for my family, to keep us in unity and good health. I focused my thoughts on the things of God and kept my mind on Him. I was determined not to spend the second half of my life as I had spent the first half. I stopped fretting over getting out, and instead learned to think only about what God would have me do from one moment to the next. I obeyed prison rules and began to care about my fellow inmates.

"Miraculously, they released me exactly two days before my first two years were up."

There are many miracles in this story. Few experts would predict that Alan could possibly change a life so habituated to drug addiction and street crime. However, my brother had been raised to believe that all things are possible with God, and he realized that without God, he could not keep himself clean. Other godly prisoners encouraged him, reminding him daily that only by God's grace and help would he make it.

Today, relocated and happily married, his life has been totally changed. Al says, "We are taking hold of the gospel plow. We cannot change where we have been, but we can change where we are going. I am rediscovering relationships within our family. Everyday activities have become such a joy—watching my son grow and watching God change my thought patterns and desires. My commitment to Him has become my main motivating force."

STUFF

Stuff you should know—One in twenty-five Americans is behind bars of America's correctional institutions. The cost to house these inmates is $2 billion a year.

I asked Alan what he'd say to another family who, despite their best efforts, finds themselves weeping for an estranged and lost son or brother. His answer was prompt.

"Trust God with that addict in your family. Believe there is hope. God hears the prayers of the righteous. I urge you never to let your heart grow cold.

"People ask me about the best way to pray for someone lost to drug addiction. I believe my mother prayed the most effective prayer of all: 'Lord, let him be caught.' If I did wrong, my mother wanted me to face the consequences. She feared that otherwise I might be lost for eternity.

"God heard her prayers, and those of many others. He hears yours, too. Remember always, the things that are impossible with man are possible with God. Trust Him."

God sets the prisoners free. In one way or another, that includes all of us. In Al's case, we had to wait a little while longer. But an old phrase reminds me of God's perfect timing: "God is rarely early. He's never late. He may not come when you want Him, but He's always on time."

Chapter 31

IMMY IMMY'S BIRTHDAY

In South America, they call Mary Martha Dabbs "Immy Immy," for M.M., the name given her by so many of her friends back home. Whatever you call her, this spunky, adventurous world traveler who grew up just outside Memphis, Tennessee, has done far more in her life than most farm girls ever dream of doing. There was the capuchin monkey she bought on the layaway plan, for example, and the way she became Elvis Presley's pen pal and friend...

But if teenaged Mary Martha enjoyed adventure, this was just a prelude to her adult life. She has journeyed to seventeen foreign countries and thirty-two of America's states. She has traveled by every means of transportation, slept on the ground and seen such wondrous sights as the Taj Mahal. In short, M.M. has done so many of the things she dreamed of as a girl—despite a lifetime of cerebral palsy and chronic pain that would have immobilized the average person.

But nobody would call Mary Martha Dabbs average. The tiny noninvalid, a lay missionary, ventures fearlessly into remote corners of the globe to carry the gospel. She returns from her travels with captivating, high-spirited stories about her adventures, misadventures and the God who goes with her into some places where most of the able-bodied might hesitate to go.

Treasure

We must never pull up in unbelief what God has planted in faith.

"On my fifth trip to Chile I was asked to speak at the church where the Chilean president attends," she told me. "I had never spoken before a group in Santiago, especially in such a huge Baptist church. At the end of the service a lady asked that someone hand me a note. It concerned the lady's niece, and she said the girl was in such terrible physical shape she was not expected to live.

"She said I should go see this girl. She didn't say 'please,' and she didn't say 'will you?' She said *go*."

It happened to be Mary Martha's birthday. The wonderful friend with whom she was staying said, "M.M., this is your day. We'll do anything you want." But Kitty, the friend, also knew about the note, and knew where the sick girl lived. She agreed to take Mary Martha to see the girl.

"The Lord had impressed on me that we should be more concerned about the needs of others than our own needs," Mary Martha explained. "I thought, *If I don't go I'll never know what God is up to.* So we went."

The two women set out to find the sick girl. On the way, M.M. prayed that they would not offend anyone in the house where they were to go. "After all, they did not know us, or know why we were there," she said. "I also prayed, 'If there is someone who does not know You, and if we lead that person to You, that will be my birthday gift to You.'"

A young man named Juan answered the door and called his mother, Eleana. She invited the two women in and offered them food. She had a little restaurant that helped to support the family. Immediately Kitty began to talk to Juan about his relationship to God. "Yes, I believe in God," Juan said. "God said, 'Welcome to the kingdom of God.' When you go to heaven some day, Jesus will be the first one to greet you."

Some time later, Kitty was driving through that little town and stopped at Juan's house with some materials M.M. wanted him to have. "I wanted to get him in the Word," she explained. "I didn't just want to leave Juan where he was; I wanted him to grow."

Juan came to the door. He was glad to see Kitty, but his first question was, "How is Immy Immy?"

The mission trips upon which Mary Martha Dabbs embarks are physically costly. Once, upon returning to the United States, she was rushed to the hospital, where she was given three cortisone shots to relieve her intense pain. When she discovered her attending physician was from India, however, she related to him immediately. At that moment thoughts of India far outweighed her physical suffering.

STUFF

The real measure of a man's wealth is not what he has invested in on earth, but what he has stored up in heaven.

"When I was a teenager I was a dreamer," M.M.

recounted. "I wanted to go to India and see the Taj Mahal. I thought, *Wouldn't it be neat if I, a farmer's daughter, could say I had seen one of the seven wonders of the world?*"

As a teenager, Mary Martha Dabbs, one of a team of twelve teenagers, had traveled to India where, despite bouts of dysentery and other difficulties, they had managed to build a church. Afterward, M.M.'s dream came true. She and her teammates were taken to see the Taj Mahal.

"Lord, thank You for allowing me to see all this beauty and perfection," she prayed, awed by the splendid sight. But God spoke to the physically limited, but spiritually limitless teenager's heart in power and in truth: "Take your eyes off man-made things, and realize I have even greater things to build for you."

Despite everything she endures, Mary Martha testifies that God's promise to her has been true. She has seen far greater evidences of love and perfection than even that of the moonlit Taj Mahal. She has seen Juan and so many other sons and daughters of God receive the gift of salvation and eternal life.

Chapter 32

HE KNOWS YOUR NAME

The pretty, vivacious young woman entered an Atlanta disco confidently. You had to know someone to get into this place. As her eyes adjusted to the lights, she felt a tap on her shoulder.

"Are you Julia?" a young man asked.

"No."

"The Lord Jesus Christ told me to come here and find a girl named Julia," the man persisted. "He wants her to come into His kingdom tonight. He told me, 'I want Julia to know that I love her.'"

"No, I am not Julia," the girl repeated, startled.

The young woman, a nominal Christian, was shaken. No one knew her by Julia, the name on her birth certificate. She'd always gone by the name Julie. *Who is that man? Was his message meant for me?* she thought. Feeling disconcerted, she left the disco immediately.

The next morning Julie woke up feeling perturbed. "My world was being shaken," she said. "I felt restless." Julie walked outside. Looking up, she said, "God, if You are real, I need to find out."

At that moment the sun shone down, and its radiance

surrounded her. The haze disappeared, and the dew instantly dried. "I phoned my girlfriend and said, 'Let's go to church tomorrow,'" Julie recalled. That decision radically changed her life.

Treasure

Faith is unutterable trust in God, trust that never dreams He will not stand by us.

By now God had her full attention. She was not even surprised at the sermon topic that day: "The Love of God." She listened intently as the pastor described the lengths to which Jesus would go to save us. "At the time, I had no clue that God was seeking me," she later said. "Two people had been praying for me. And now I believe God sent an angel into that disco to seek me out. I had never seen that man before, and I never saw him again."

By the end of the church service, Julie had become convinced that God knew her name—*Julia*. She knew He had called her, and that day she answered. She had little knowledge of the Bible at that point, and did not know Isaiah 43:1, where God says, "Fear not, for I have redeemed you; I have called you by your name; you are Mine."

Even at age eighteen, Julie had her future mapped out. The energetic beauty meant to go places. She intended to work for one of America's corporate giants, an Atlanta-based operation, moving right up the ladder in corporate headquarters. She intended to become rich and, of course, eventually to marry an equally wealthy and successful man.

Those lofty ambitions took a back seat, however, as Julie entered into her new Christian lifestyle. Discovering the riches of the Bible...learning how amazingly prayer changes things...meeting other ardently enthusiastic young people who were seeking God's plan for their lives...all of it excited her.

At an informal church singles' function at her college and career pastor's home, Julie conversed with the musician who would accompany their function. He was an interesting guy, she thought, a college student who possessed unusual presence. He could play and sing any gospel song. What's more, his favorite secular group was Earth, Wind and Fire, which was Julie's favorite. His name? Paul Dana Walker, the son of Dr. Paul L. Walker, Julie's pastor.

They made a dynamic pair. Paul Dana's exceptional scholastic, athletic and musical abilities made it clear this young man also was going places. But his heart, Julie immediately discovered, was strongly committed to a life of Christian service. Serious as Paul Dana's life direction might be, however, she also found him as fun-loving as herself. They drank gallons of coffee together, ate pounds of cheesecake and talked. Their marriage seemed inevitable, predestined.

"It was a match made in heaven," Julie declares. "We had fun, but we could disagree. I chose to leave all my ambitions behind me. My life was becoming fuller, more wonderful, than anything I'd ever imagined."

When Paul Dana graduated college with highest honors, he was offered a teaching post at Lee College in Cleveland, Tennessee. On November 29, 1980, the couple's future seemed assured. They were eager to move to Cleveland and assume their new roles. Early that Saturday morning, however, their plans and lives became shattered instantly in a horrifying highway crash.

Julie woke up in an Atlanta hospital. She went through hours of surgery, as doctors frantically tried to stabilize her and performed life-saving procedures. Thousands of people went into prayer. No one felt optimistic about the youthful widow's chances for survival.

After coming out of surgery, Julie was told, "We have bad news and worse news. You have many broken bones. You have internal injuries. Your face is badly damaged."

The barely conscious girl responded, "If that's the worse news, what's the bad news?"

"No, that was the bad news." There was the longest pause in the world, and then the words came. "The worse news is, Paul Dana is dead."

Grief and heartbreak swirled around her as an entire church community felt the deep loss of one of its most promising sons, and the pastor's family endured the weight of crushing sorrow.

"Only someone as young, strong and resilient as Julie could have survived," one church member said. "Her injuries alone were devastating, but the loss of Paul Dana was unbearable for all of us."

Julie says, "Going through this with Christ was a lot better—walking hand in hand with a loving God—than if I'd had to walk alone with no hope."

Months of healing ensued before Julie actually could physically walk. Sometimes she rebelled at the pain and the casts, even as she humbly realized that for her, life itself had become a miracle. And when her unthinkable physical and emotional injuries had healed enough, spunky Julie enrolled in Lee College where she and Paul Dana should have been, where Julie should have been a professor's wife. She vigorously pursued her academic career—and graduated.

"Just as I thought I was coming out of it, putting my life back together, my brother-in-law Mark came into my room, knelt down beside me and said, 'Julie, I have some horrible news. Your brother has died.'

"We sat there and sobbed," she said.

For a time, Julie felt total numbness and isolation. She

STUFF

I seek God first when I am weak... I need God most when I think I'm strong.

says the only hope she had, the only thing she felt she had left, was Jesus Christ. "During that long desert experience God began teaching me things," she realizes. "He taught me how to love again. He reminded me that He is my rod and my staff. He helped me return to the fact that His Word is truth and life.

"One day, years after his death, I went to Paul Dana's grave and talked to him," Julie related. "I played an Earth, Wind and Fire piece, then knelt and talked to Paul. I told him it was time for me to move on. I said, 'I love you, but I'm going now.'"

Julie left the gravesite, feeling a mixture of sadness and

anticipation. At that poignant moment, just as she entered the expressway, she heard someone in a passing car call out...

"Julie! Julie Walker!"

Incredulous, she looked around, to see a young man motioning her to pull off the highway. The two of them parked alongside the traffic-heavy road.

"I'm Emory. Remember me?"

"Yes, but I don't date."

"I didn't ask you for a date," the man said. Julie thought he was the handsomest man.

"No, but I just wanted to get that out..."

"And I just wanted to say hello," he added.

He had called her by name. At the most inopportune time, at the strangest moment and amidst needle-in-the-haystack traffic, Emory had seen her and called her by her name.

Emory Crews and Julie Walker-Crews have been married for seventeen years now and have three children. Recently, she and her husband attended a concert by Earth, Wind and Fire.

"Unexpectedly, that night I met Verdine White," she said. "We brought Paul Dana's bass for him to autograph, and I shared with him Paul's admiration for his musical abilities and Paul's life as a preacher. With sincere gladness, Verdine signed the bass—a dream come true after many years waiting. Only God could have orchestrated that moment.

"That night I realized God had brought me through our desert experiences to reach the other side. He showed me that night, 'Julie, the scars on your face remain as a living memorial for all I have done for you. Remember, I called you by your name; you are Mine.' He is risen; He is risen indeed."

As it is written in Isaiah 43:1–3:

> Fear not, for I have redeemed you; I have called you by your name; you are Mine. When you pass through the waters, I will be with you; and through the rivers, they shall not overflow you. When you walk through the fire, you shall not be burned, nor shall the flame scorch you. For I am the Lord your God.

Chapter 33

A NOT-SO-ORDINARY PERSON

We all know at least one magnificent champion, someone who becomes a lifelong source of inspiration. I met mine in an amazing way. On a brilliant, late-summer Michigan day, I was one of countless students standing in seemingly unending registration lines to enroll at Spring Arbor College in Spring Arbor, Michigan.

As a junior transferring from my former community college, Spring Arbor was not my first choice. I had applied to several secular schools closer to Detroit and Motown Records, and I had auditioned for scholarships, hoping to be accepted at a school that could serve as a springboard for my musical ambitions. But it was quaint Spring Arbor College that had accepted my application, awarded me scholarship monies and later would challenge me to a greater Christian faith and commitment.

Grateful for the school's acceptance, I nevertheless had mixed feelings about the way things had turned out. Obviously my career ambitions would be slowed until after I earned my degree. But little could I have imagined, standing with other students in line that day, that I was about to meet someone who would change my life forever and become the catalyst for my future career and ministry.

As my line in the college fieldhouse inched forward, I found myself standing next to a table on which the college radio station had placed bins of used records for sale. I browsed through the long-playing albums, not really intending to buy—until one cover grabbed my attention. A very young and pretty Black singer, seated in a wicker chair, seemed to smile directly into my eyes. Her name was Danniebelle Hall, and I had never heard of her. Though I was not familiar with her music, something about that album intrigued me, and I bought it.

In His unusual way, God had just intersected time and place, and He was about to use one special person to change a life...mine. Isn't it funny that none of this happened in the way I might have imagined it would?

I took my new record album home and placed the disc on my turntable. Fresh, contemporary melodies and innovative lyrics leaped out into the room and immediately held me spellbound. I'd never heard music like this before! Danniebelle's voice quality was unlike anyone else's, a signature to her gap-toothed smile. God used Danniebelle Hall's music to arrest me. If my heart was a bull's-eye, her music was the arrow. I became forever changed.

You have to realize, contemporary Christian music at that time was in its infancy. Growing up in a small town and a very traditional church that loved what I considered old-fashioned gospel music, I'd had no access to music as bright and innovative as this. Though I was looking for an alternative to the sounds I'd heard all my life, I also was seeking what seemed impossible...a place, an identity, for a young, Black, contemporary woman who sang alto and played the piano.

That's why I had gravitated to the music of Aretha Franklin, Roberta Flack, the Supremes and Martha Reeves and the Vandellas. I felt I had no choice but to pursue a career in secular music. No Christian music seemed to match my voice, my outlook and my style...until I heard Danniebelle Hall.

So I mimicked her vocal style. I copied her piano licks.

Treasure

There are lessons that can only be learned along the road of affliction, hardship and pain.
—Charles Swindoll

I began singing her songs on campus and around town in special appearances. She gave me something powerful to sing and say. What I did not recognize at the time, however, was that God was using her, along with my fellow students at the college He had chosen for me to attend, to lead me straight into the firm, unshakable, adult Christian commitment that undergirds my ministry today.

At first I knew Danniebelle Hall through her music and the pretty face on a black-and-white album cover. It was some time before I met her and learned her story. As the fourth of eight children whose parents had to struggle to support them, she was placed with foster parents. The elderly couple had health problems; in fact, the man was blind.

Nevertheless, Danniebelle's foster parents recognized her

talents and saw that she took piano lessons. She had to practice thirty minutes a day on the family's old upright piano, always prepared to make a swift getaway to join her waiting friends. She practiced piano with her roller skates on.

Like me, Danniebelle grew up in the church. The church mothers, older women in the Pentecostal storefront church she attended, nurtured and cared for bright little Danniebelle, who excelled in her studies. She loved music and languages, and she recalls with affection that her father's love for foreign languages influenced her greatly.

Mama Carter, her devoted foster mother, had some special bonding with Danniebelle in the kitchen, where on Saturdays the two would always make homemade rolls. Danniebelle says she never could figure out why her dough always looked a little dirty and never quite rose to the occasion. However, that began her lifelong love of the kitchen and cooking.

In 1969, Danniebelle Hall moved from the East Coast to California and became church musician for a Los Angeles congregation. From there, she began ministering in music throughout the state. Eventually she met musician and song-writer Audrey Meir, who composed "His Name Is Wonderful" and other favorites.

Danniebelle calls Audrey her Polish-Irish mother. It was Audrey who suggested that she send a tape of her singing to a young writer and singer named Andrae Crouch. This turned out to be a life-changing move for both artists. Danniebelle felt impressed with Andrae's cordial personality, the way he would chat with his audience before his concerts began. She was affected by his genuine rapport with people and the way he welcomed others as part of his family.

Eventually Danniebelle became one of the singers in Andrae Crouch's noted singing group, the Disciples. She says traveling with the renowned gospel great taught her much, and opportunities increased. Many lives were greatly touched by this group...including that of a young Babbie Mason, who had followed Danniebelle's course and watched her become an outstanding figure on the Christian music scene.

Such ministry frequently becomes physically exhausting, however. Danniebelle Hall recalls one year in which she and the Disciples traveled with Andrae Crouch for two hundred sixty nights, performing "one-nighters" across America. She cautions other musicians to place their family first, knowing from experience that families suffer when a mother is away that much.

Upon launching her solo career, however, the artist found herself traveling around the globe. Nigeria and Sweden are highlights of her travels, she says. Meanwhile, I continued to keep up with the songs she was writing—such powerful new music as "Ordinary People," "Turn It Over to Jesus," "Theme on the Thirty-Seventh" and her renditions of such favorite hymns as "Great Is Thy Faithfulness."

Anyone who knows me can see how much this Christian singer, musician and songwriter has influenced my own career and calling. It's easy enough to understand why this powerful woman became a champion in my sight. Yet few know the rest of the story.

If Danniebelle Hall's tremendous influence on today's Christian music guided and inspired me, her shining faith and example amidst trials inspire me even more.

Today, the woman who has traveled, sung and ministered

throughout the world is confined to a wheelchair. By no means elderly, Danniebelle already has weathered tremendous storms. She has endured breast cancer and a mastectomy, has lost a leg and battles kidney failure through dialysis four times each week.

But Danniebelle prevails! She radiates confidence that God has a plan for her at this stage of her life, her music and her ministry. In the assisted-living community in which she lives, the woman who has ministered to audiences of thousands now serves her one hundred twenty housemates. Younger than most of the other residents, buoyant Danniebelle galvanizes others to participate in the weekly Bible studies she hosts. She also conducts prayer meetings and memorial services for those who, as she puts it, make their last move.

STUFF

Interesting stuff— Listening to music can reduce stress by as much as 41 percent.

Danniebelle acts as mediator, counselor and champion checker player, admonishing senior residents to make their peace with God and live together as neighbors. She sees her special community as her personal mission field. She introduces her music to her neighbors, who listen and enjoy it. Carrying her portable keyboard to the in-house worship services, she offers constant hope and encouragement to those who are lonely or in desperate need, physically and emotionally.

My champion, mentor and mother in the ministry,

Danniebelle Hall, faces life as a cheerleader and warrior. I see her as a pioneer, a trailblazer, someone who cannot be defeated. She refuses to become a victim. She wrings all the juices out of life. Her rounded face and wide eyes, her famous gap-toothed smile, show the world she's still determined to keep on showing up.

She presses on, using a wheelchair and traveling in a van with a hydraulic lift. She keeps a constant song in her heart, no matter how tough the battles.

How can anyone still so young continue to face such daunting difficulties so gallantly? I asked Danniebelle that question, and she answered with two scripture verses:

> For I know the thoughts and plans that I have for you, says the Lord, thoughts and plans for welfare and peace and not for evil, to give you hope in your final outcome.
>
> —JEREMIAH 29:11, AMP

> And I am convinced and sure of this very thing, that He Who began a good work in you will continue until the day of Jesus Christ [right up to the time of His return], developing [that good work] and perfecting and bringing it to full completion in you.
>
> —PHILIPPIANS 1:6, AMP

Those two strong verses describe the strong faith in my favorite champion, a not-so-ordinary person—Danniebelle Hall. So do her closing words during our recent conversation. "All is well," that familiar voice declared. "All is well!"

Section III

~

GOD'S PRESENCE

Sometimes we find ourselves in trouble; sometimes trouble finds us. Either way, our situations often appear too big for us to handle. An old adage says, "God helps those who help themselves." But God's track record proves that He always helps those who *cannot* help themselves. These compelling stories remind us that God is as close as our next breath. When we call on Him, He shows up as the . . .

Miracle-worker in our mess.

Chapter 34

SPEAK, LORD

My husband, Charles, and I have tried to instill concepts of responsibility into our children from an early age. When our younger son was in grade school, he already had known our rules concerning his responsibilities for several years.

The rules were simple. The moment he came home from school, he must complete his chores and do his homework. Chores included taking out the trash, feeding the dog and straightening his room. Those chores had to be completed before he engaged in leisure activities.

One day after school, our son rushed into the house, headed for the television set and immediately began to play a new video game he'd received for Christmas. In the kitchen preparing dinner, I waited for my son to empty the overflowing trash can. Instead, blaring from the family room at deafening levels, I heard music and sound effects from the video game.

"What does it take to get my child to accept responsibility, walk in obedience and take out the trash without being told?" I asked myself in some exasperation.

So I went through the familiar routine. I called to him

from the kitchen, raising my voice a little bit. No answer. I called again, louder this time. Again, no answer. Finally, I assumed the stance every mother in the world uses at one time or another. Hands on hips, with a really firm voice, I called my son a third time.

Treasure

The more faithfully you listen to the voice within you, the better you will hear what is sounding outside.
—Dag Hammarskjold

This time, I called him by his first, middle and last names, followed by a threat to do bodily harm. This got a response! He presented himself in the kitchen, where I proceeded to begin a really incisive lecture—when suddenly a light turned on in my head.

In an instant, profound moment, I knew my lecture was dying even before it had a chance to begin. *It was going to be such a good lecture, too . . .*

But the Holy Spirit interrupted me with something He wanted *me* to hear and learn. I stood in my tracks, stunned, as I "heard" these words come from Him. "How many times have I called you and gotten no answer? How many times have I tried to get your attention, with still no answer? How many times have I had to resort to extreme measures to get your attention?"

I stood speechless in my kitchen as the voice of the Holy Spirit called me by my first, middle and last names with those words of correction. I excused my child, chuckled at the Holy Spirit's teaching techniques and sat down to ponder these thoughts and apply them to my life.

I recently heard a phrase that has stuck with me: "Lord, now that You've taken me out of Egypt, please take Egypt out of me." If I allow it, the noise of the world floods in. I get preoccupied with trivial matters that crowd out God's voice. Circumstances concern me, and I don't understand His instruction. Anxiety begins

STUFF

Good stuff—One sincere apology is worth more than all the roses money can buy.

to consume me, so I am tempted to worry and not to pray. Distractions lure me, so sometimes I don't heed the Spirit's admonishments when He calls me with words of warning. Because of my disobedience, I behave like Adam when God called to him in the Garden. Same response. Different offense.

"I heard You, but I was doing something I had no business doing."

Having ears attuned to God's voice—and spirits willing to obey that voice—is vital not only for instruction, but also for intimacy and fellowship with Him. At times God may speak through thunder and lightening. His voice may echo through the mountains or over the ocean waves. Other times He speaks in a whisper or a nudge, through the wind, a song or His written word.

I desire to be like a boy named Samuel. Samuel teaches us the importance of becoming a good listener, one who can hear and obey God. The first time he heard God's voice,

Samuel rose from his bed with a heart that was ready and willing to obey. He went to the priest Eli three times. Finally, the priest instructed Samuel, "If the voice calls again, say 'Speak, Lord. Your servant hears.'" (See 1 Samuel 3:1–11.)

What a great lesson to learn. God desires that you and I walk so closely with Him that we can hear Him, in a breath, utter our name. He is pleased when we answer Him immediately, without reservation.

Is there so much noise in your life that our heavenly Father has to shout over it or call you by all of your names to get your attention? Must He resort to extreme measures? Does He have to repeat His call often, or reiterate a lesson you should have learned in the past?

Now is a good time to ask for the Holy Spirit's help in those areas where you are lacking. What does the Lord want to teach you? What does He desire to tell you? Pull away for a quiet moment today and say to the Lord, "Speak, Lord. Your servant hears."

Chapter 35

STANDING IN THE GAP

As a young girl in my pastor-father's church, often I heard older members of our congregation say to others going through trying circumstances, "Don't worry. God is in control. Remember, *I'm standing in the gap for you.*"

I didn't know much about prayer then, but my intuition told me that standing in the gap was a different kind of prayer. It meant serious, aggressive, intercessory prayer. It would take many years, trying situations and inspiration from the Holy Spirit in the area of songwriting before I'd begin to understand better what the phrase "standing in the gap" means. It took one of my son's football games to paint a picture I'll not soon forget.

Jerry, our older son, was about ten when he earned a spot on the neighborhood football team. (It helped to have Dad as coach.) Now, I enjoy watching professional football teams on television, but I am constantly aware of the sport's dangers. So conscious, in fact, that I can hardly enjoy the game. So you can imagine how nervous I'd get at our son's Saturday morning football games.

The season was going well. The team was advancing, and

since Jerry looked pretty good on the field that day, my husband decided to let him play quarterback. I was proud to watch our boy use strategy and maneuver about the field.

Treasure

If the world is cold, make it your business to build fires.
—Horace Trauble

However, a certain play turned my fears into reality. The ball was hiked to Jerry. He looked for an open man to receive the pass, but before he could release the ball, he got sacked. Seconds later, the entire opposition piled on top of my son in a huge heap.

After the dust settled and the smoke cleared, everyone got off the field—except Jerry. He lay motionless. My husband and the coaching staff hurried to him. They knelt around him, doing whatever coaches do when a man is down on the field, but Jerry didn't move. They began administering whatever it is that they administer, and still I saw no response.

At that moment an overwhelming sense of mothering came over me, and I believe I reacted as any right-minded mother would react. As if some outside force were propelling me, I got out of my seat and shot toward the field. Before I knew it, I was making a mad dash for the thirty-yard line. The coaches must have seen the look in my eye. You know, that look that says, "Step aside, boys. This momma means business." They parted like the Red Sea.

I knelt on the field next to my son, laid my hands on him

and prayed aloud: "In the name of Jesus, you *will* rise up from this field, and you *will* walk again." Only moments later, the miracle happened. Jerry looked up at me through the mask of his helmet and called my name.

"Momma. MOMMA! GET OFF THE FIELD!"

I felt not the least bit fazed by what he said, only joy and gratitude that he spoke to me. I got up, brushed off my jeans, wiped my hands and returned to the bleachers. *Another mission accomplished, another prayer answered,* I thought.

That football incident caused me to see and understand better what "standing in the gap" really means. I realized this is what the people of God, the church, must do for one another. The church is not a museum for dead saints—it is a hospital for sinners. When my son was down on the field, without thinking twice, seemingly all in one motion, I swung into action.

I ran onto the field, knelt in the mud and called out to God, our very present help in time of trouble. In that same way, the body of Christ must willingly get down on her knees, sometimes get her hands dirty, sometimes become inconvenienced, in order to counsel, reach out a hand and offer a compassionate embrace.

The church is to bend her back to lift a brother out of his pit. Fellow believers are to rise to their feet and journey alongside that sister who is friendless and alone. Intercessors must raise their voices and call out to God for those who are defenseless and hurting.

How ridiculous it would have been had I rushed out to the field, pointed a long finger of judgment in my child's face and said, "If you had watched where you were going, none of this would have happened. Had you walked where you should, you would have spared us a lot of pain and embarrassment. But because you were so careless and weak, we are going to alienate you, disassociate ourselves from you and kick you off the team!"

How ludicrous that sounds! But too many times the body of Christ administers judgment instead of healing. We ostracize and criticize hurting brothers and sisters whom we should be building up and encouraging. So many Christians are wounded because of the *reaction*, not the *response*, of the church. Yes, Christians make mistakes. But love covers a multitude of sins. (See Proverbs 10:12.) Besides, who among us would be first in line to throw stones? (See John 8:7.)

Standing in the gap means bearing the infirmities of the weak and lifting those who have fallen. Yes, we're even called to feel their pain. That is exactly what Christ has done for us. The Bible says, "For when we were still without strength, in due time Christ died for the ungodly" Rom. 5:6). Even now, Christ stands in the gap for you and me.

Romans 8:27 tells us that Jesus makes intercession for us before the Father. Isn't it comforting to know that Jesus intercedes for you and me right now? He is praying for our health, strength, family, marriage, finances and everything else that concerns us. Right now He sits at the right hand of the Father, calling out your name. And if anyone can get a prayer answered, Jesus can!

Have you ever felt that life has sneaked up from behind, tackled you like a linebacker from the Green Bay Packers, thrown you to the ground and left you there, unable to move? Has some situation at home shocked you to the core and left you feeling numb and lifeless? Those are the times when we need a member of the body of Christ to rush out on life's playing field, lay hands on us and say, "In the name of Jesus, you *will* rise up, and you *will* walk again." We need someone to take us by the hand and walk with us on our uphill journey. We need someone who will stand in the gap for us, someone who will take up the slack, pray when we cannot find the words, bear our load and lift us when we fall.

Standing in the gap means holding up a brother or sister when that person is too weak to stand. A perfect illustration of that occurs in Exodus 17:12. The children of Israel were at war with the Amalekites. God instructed Moses to lift up the rod to assure the Israelites' victory. But Moses' arms soon became too heavy, too weary, to hold the rod aloft. His arms came down, and the Israelites were defeated.

But that's where Aaron and Hur came in. They sat Moses on a huge rock. With Aaron on one side and Hur on the other, Moses leaned into and gained strength from his close friends. When Moses could no longer lift his own arms, Aaron and Hur stood in the gap. They lifted his arms, and the people of God became victorious.

STUFF

Don't cry about stuff you can change.
—Bishop T. D. Jakes

Just before I wrote the song "Standing in the Gap," I discovered Ezekiel 22:30. The twenty-second chapter of Ezekiel reads like the front page of today's newspaper: Crimes, government corruption, disrespect for parents and idol worship were rampant. In verse 30, God says, "I sought for a man among them who would make a wall, and stand in the gap before Me on behalf of the land, that I should not destroy it; but I found no one."

No one was praying a divine hedge of protection around the city to keep the people safe and the enemy at bay. (See Job 1:10.) No one was interceding for the people, for their families and children. No one was calling on God for forgiveness of sins. What a wake-up call for the church today!

Has God spoken to you about standing in the gap for our country's leaders, churches, homes and schools? Do you know someone who needs some of your strength today? Has the Holy Spirit prompted you to pray a hedge of protection around someone who is walking through the valley?

Perhaps He is nudging you to write a note or place a phone call to someone you know who is lonely. Or maybe you could prepare a meal, clothe someone, pay a neighbor's light bill or care for her children. That's what gap-standers do. They make the first move too, knowing the one needing help may be too weak, discouraged or embarrassed to ask.

The church needs you and me. We—like Moses, Aaron and Hur—are called to stand in the gap for others. Trials and tribulations, like storms, are inevitable in this life. Either we are in them, coming out of them or headed for them. We must stand in the gap for our brother or sister because we know that it won't be long before we'll need someone to stand in the gap for us. As the older members of my father's church would say, "If it ain't one thing, it's another."

I'm still singing the words to a song the Lord helped me write several years ago. Hopefully, it will encourage you.

> I'll be standing in the gap for you.
> Just remember, someone, somewhere,
> Is praying for you
> Calling out your name,
> Praying for your strength.
> I'll be standing in the gap for you.[1]

---

[1] "Standing in the Gap" by Babbie Mason. Copyright © 1994 by May Sun Music and Word Music, Inc. All rights reserved. Used by permission. International rights secured.

Chapter 36

ON THIN ICE

My brother Ben, a Michigan pastor, claims he has an addiction almost too powerful to shake—ice fishing. Pastor Ben Wade is passionate about the sport, noting that there's no Ice-fishing Persons Anonymous or other support group for people like him.

But one cold day a few seasons ago, Ben learned...far out on the ice as the sun was going down...that indeed he did have support. I'll let him tell his story.

> For people hooked, as I am, on ice fishing, our salvation lies in the fact that the lakes stay frozen only from late December until the end of March. I'm not one to take chances. Only when I see fishing shanties and snowmobiles on the frozen lake do I feel safe in venturing out. However, the experienced ice fisherman knows the season's best fishing arrives at "first ice" or "last ice."
>
> A few seasons ago on Clark Lake, the black crappie were fourteen and fifteen inches long, and bluegills (we call 'em breem back home) averaged about ten inches. I'm convinced heaven will have ice fishing. I'm hoping to be raptured with ice augur in hand, so I may cut a hole in that crystal sea and wet a line!

A few winters ago, fishing was great and the weather cooperated wonderfully. Winter hung on until early April. Some days would warm up into the forties, but nighttime temperatures would dip well below freezing and preserve that ice and keep it safe for fishing.

One April evening, realizing my ice-fishing days were numbered, I rushed home from work, threw my gear in the truck and hurriedly dressed in cold-weather garb as I headed for the door. I yelled good-bye to my wife and headed for the lake.

The warming weather had melted most of the snow on the ice and left puddles standing in spots. This standing water causes honey-combed ice, which can be deceptive and dangerous. I picked my way carefully, going from snow-covered patch to snow-covered patch, paying attention so I could follow my tracks on returning.

When I reached my favorite spot, the fish cooperated, and I realized that for the time being, this might be as close to heaven as I could get.

Then suddenly, it occurred to me that I was the only person left on the lake. Two guys had been fishing nearby, but now their retreating figures headed toward shore in the quickly failing evening light. They moved slowly, cautiously. One stopped and lit a lantern, then they continued. The one carrying the light must have slipped on a slick spot on the ice, because I heard glass breaking, The light went out, and there was angry swearing. The guy had fallen on the ice.

I picked up my Coleman lantern as the sun dipped

behind the tree-lined horizon, and was thankful for the light. The fish were still biting, but I reluctantly began packing up. Maybe we'll get one more night of hard freeze so there would be one last day of safe fishing, I thought.

Darkness fell. It was like dropping a curtain. Quickly I packed my gear and looked for my footprints, which would guide me to shore. Suddenly, my lantern sputtered out. In my haste, I had neglected to fill it!

> ## Treasure
>
> *Go as far as you can see. When you get there, you will be able to see farther.*
> —*Thomas Carlyle*

It was dark. I was alone. I knew it was some two hundred yards to shore, with no lights—two hundred dangerous yards. The water was nearly twenty feet deep where I had been fishing. For more than half the distance to shore, icy water would be well over my head.

I stopped walking. I prayed. Not an Old Testament, King James Version prayer, no eloquence, no thoughtful choice of phrase. With face turned to heaven, I cried out three words: "God, help me!"

Still facing toward heaven, I opened my eyes to see the wind pushing the clouds across the sky. The clouds seemed to rush past. As I continued to watch the heavens, God unveiled a full moon, which shone so brightly that it perfectly revealed the patches of snow that could lead me safely to shore. It continued to shine as I gingerly picked my way across the thawing lake from snow patch to snow patch, until I reached safety.

Grateful and awed, I threw my fishing gear in the truck and said aloud, "Thank You, Lord." Then I guaranteed Him that He would never again have to answer that prayer!

At times we find ourselves on thin ice. Sometimes it's all we can do to cry out just three words: "God, help me!"

But He is with us. He hears us. And He can move the wind, the clouds, the moon, heaven and earth—or send legions of angels, if needed, to save one of His own.

STUFF

Ice freezes from the top down and thaws from the bottom up.

"God, help me!" That is a powerful prayer that our all-powerful God answers more times than any of us will ever know. He loves you, hears you and will save you to the uttermost.

Chapter 37

∽

OLD TREASURES

When it comes to antique stores, my car seems to have a mind of its own. Without a second thought, I somehow find myself pulling into parking lots of old warehouses, quaintly decorated bungalows or crowded storefronts on small town squares.

There's something about old finds—their colors, scents, the fact that they have endured—that draws me to them. One day, as I drove back to Atlanta from the songwriting class I teach at Lee University in Cleveland, Tennessee, I spotted a store that looked interesting. I decided to stop.

Browsing through its crowded aisles looking for anything charming, whimsical or appealing, I found myself wondering, *Was that contraption once used in an office or a barn? How many deviled eggs have been served on that Tiara amber glassware? Did the owner of*

Treasure

The power of God's love set to words or music remains timeless.

those gold wire-rimmed spectacles love the Lord? Did he read the Bible by lamplight?

Nothing seemed to insist that I take it home, however, so I moved slowly toward the front door. Then, in my peripheral view, I spotted a leather-bound book perched atop a stack of old schoolbooks. As I gravitated toward the volume, I took note: *Excellent condition, leather binding, gold-stamped title . . .*

The worn cover carried the title *The Psalmist*. Handling it carefully, I turned to the title pages. Copyright 1843! Eagerly, I thumbed through the pages, yellowed by the years, to find the most beautiful words to hundreds of the church's oldest hymns. There were no music notations, only the lofty thoughts and stately verses written by long-dead men and women who worshiped God.

Some of the words were familiar to me, but most were now part of America's early church history. My feet seemed glued to the floor. I stood, speechless, devouring the beauty I held in my hands. *These hymns were so well loved and familiar once,* I thought, *that they had no titles—only numbers.* Number 535 read:

> This world would be a wilderness
> If banished, Lord, from Thee;
> And heaven, without Thy smiling face,
> Would be no Heaven to me.
>
> My Friend Thou art where'er I go
> The object of my love
> My kind Protector here below
> And my reward above.

When foes intrude or tyrants frown
Thou art my sure relief
To Thee I make my sorrows known
And tell Thee all my grief.

'Midst rising winds and beating storms
Reclining on Thy breast
I find in Thee a hiding place,
And there securely rest.

Then I read another, hymn number 244:

Now for a tune of lofty praise
To Great Jehovah's equal Son.
Awake, my voice, in Heavenly lays,
And tell the wonders He hath done.

See how He left the worlds of light
And those bright robes He wore above;
How swift and joyful was His flight
On wings of everlasting love!

Deep in the shades of gloomy death
The eternal Captive prisoner lay;
The almighty Captive left the earth,
And rose to everlasting day.

Among a thousand harps and songs,
Jesus, the God, exalted reigns;
His sacred name fills all our tongues,
And echoes through the heavenly plains.

It may have been an antiques store, but God's presence was there. I felt that I was standing on holy ground, surrounded by a Presence far more ancient than anything else that dusty space could contain, One who is everlasting among the crumbling relics in that shop.

His presence, I thought, is priceless beyond the most splendid heirlooms lovingly passed down through generations, more splendid even than the billions of dazzling stars He created to glitter in millions of brilliant midnights.

His presence, richer than the finest tapestries, woven for royalty and carefully preserved, yet insignificant beside His beautiful world with its mountains and valleys, fields and streams, and people of every race and color.

His presence spoke eternity into time, breathed life into man and saved a wretch like me.

STUFF

In too many churches we worship our work, we work at our play and we play at our worship.

At that moment, the presence of God reminded me again that before I was conceived, He knew me by name, and He loved me.

The power of God's love set to words or music remains timeless. It transcends centuries and generations, races and cultures. It melts the hardest of hearts. From the hearts of the church's finest hymn writers, through the pages upon which those words are written, come eternal principles to remind the believer that our God is sovereign, timeless and almighty.

Sometime soon, I hope you will read through some of the

great old hymns, as I love to do since I found that wonderful antique songbook. In Zephaniah 3:17, the Bible tells us: "The LORD your God in your midst, the Mighty One, will save; He will rejoice over you with gladness, He will quiet you with His love, He will rejoice over you with singing."

Read the hymns godly men and women have penned across the centuries. Stop a moment, and hopefully you will hear God, in all His delight, singing over you.

Chapter 38

DADDY'S LITTLE GIRL

I can still see him…always on a mission, long, lanky legs, purposeful stride and wide gait, greeting his world with a wide-eyed smile. His world always smiled back. He never met a stranger he wouldn't befriend or a challenge he couldn't conquer.

It has been thirteen years, and I still miss my father. The day I received the news of his passing, I felt as if my heart had been yanked from my body, leaving a huge hole in my chest that actually hurt for a long, long time. The pain has subsided, but tears still flow easily.

As pastor of a fledgling church in its infancy, my father, with my mother and a tiny band of believers, saw it grow consistently for four decades until Daddy's heart gave out and he went home to be with Jesus. During those years, I saw my father pour his life into the church. His actions demonstrated that he knew the church was not just a building, but the people who gathered there. He shared his insatiable passion for God's Word and shepherded a congregation that grew to a like passion.

Daddy was never off duty. We had family vacations, but were always home by Saturday, in time to rest and prepare for Sunday worship. Nothing interfered with our responsibility to the church. I don't remember ever seeing my father wear jeans or tennis shoes. He even fished in dress pants, hard-soled shoes and a dress hat. His work was not a job, but a lifestyle.

As Daddy strode purposefully through our house, we usually heard him mumbling—and knew he was preaching his next sermon. As a Black pastor during the Civil Rights Movement, he rallied his church and community to register and vote for change. He instilled confidence into people who historically had been stripped of nearly everything, including their dignity.

Treasure

Every daughter of God should believe she is her Father's best girl, and that she holds a special place in Daddy's heart.

People depended on my father. I think of the night when one old gentleman telephoned late, complaining that he was experiencing some physical discomfort. Elderly and embarrassed, he was not comfortable with the idea of going to the hospital emergency room. Instead, he called his pastor.

Daddy made a recommendation and instructed him to call back when he felt better. A couple of hours later, the old deacon phoned to report that his discomfort had passed (pun intended).

Growing up, I never heard Daddy complain about how much people depended on him. A man with tremendous purpose and vision, always kind and caring, I never recall his raising his voice except in the pulpit. Well, maybe he yelled once or twice at my older brother, but I'm sure he needed it. I know Daddy wasn't perfect, but in my eyes he could do no wrong.

Pastor, teacher, college professor, chaplain, county commissioner, advisor, friend, fisherman and fisher of men...all things to all people, Daddy wore his titles well. But the one title that means most to me is *father*.

Theologians say the quality of our relationship with God, our heavenly Father, relates directly to that with our earthly father. God desires kinship with us, the kind of fellowship a father has with his children.

What an awesome privilege! The almighty, holy God and Judge of the Old Testament, whose name, out of fear, could not be spoken, suddenly reveals Himself in a whole new light in the Gospels of the New Testament. Jesus called God "Father" more than any other name. He taught us to pray, "Our Father."

Jesus pleaded with His Father in the Garden of Gethsemane. He cried out to His Father during His crucifixion. He prayed to His Father at Lazarus' resurrection. Jesus demonstrated that our relationship with God is *intimate and personal*.

God exhibits every quality of the perfect Father. He loves us with an everlasting love. He thinks of us all the time. He has prepared for our future. He is strong and powerful, able to protect us from all danger. He is tender, compassionate and concerned when we are hurting, and He assures us that not even one of our concerns escapes His notice.

God is our provider, sure to anticipate and meet our every need, even before we know we need it. His love is satisfying and complete. Nothing can replace it. He knows our name. He knows where we live. He cares about the tiniest, apparently most insignificant details of our lives.

But you may say, "My father never was like that." For many of us, the word *father* has become associated with fear, anger, absence, neglect or abuse. It's true that earthly fathers can be mean-spirited, unpredictable or uncaring. Some of your childhood memories of your father might be painful.

Maybe you never met your real father, or don't even know his name. Because of this, it's easy to have a distorted view of who God really is. That is why God sent His Son, Jesus, to show us what God looks like. If we really want to know God, we must see Him as Jesus saw Him. As Jesus walked on earth, His life was consumed with a satisfying love relationship with His heavenly Father.

Are you a daddy's girl? When you think of a daddy's girl, what do you see? My mind's eye offers a picture of a father teaching his little girl to dance. With her tiny hand in his, they glide across the floor in perfect step. She does not worry about making a misstep or getting crushed under her dad's big foot.

The dad already thought about that. He teaches his little girl to follow his steps by placing her little feet on top of his big shoes so she will not miss a beat.

Or I think of a dad as he walks his daughter down the aisle on her wedding day, wanting to hold on, yet giving her away.

I picture my own dad, baiting my cane fishing pole with a squirmy nightcrawler, tossing the line from the boat, helping me watch the red-and-white bobber and instructing me when to pull in the line. He'd take the fish off my hook and start the whole process over again. Somehow, I guess, he got to enjoy some fishing, too. But that's what dads do. They put the needs of their children ahead of their own.

As the church pianist, starting my full-time responsibilities at age nine, I served during all the Sunday services and several choir rehearsals during the week. Since I spent a lot of time involved in my father's ministry, I always considered myself Daddy's favorite.

My younger sister begs to differ. For her own reasons, she'd say she was Daddy's favorite daughter. For one thing, she always thought she was Daddy's favorite because she bears a striking resemblance to our mother.

STUFF

Interesting stuff— The daughters of Muhammed Ali, Joe Frazier and George Foreman followed in their father's footsteps and entered the ring as professional boxers.

But isn't that the way it should be? Shouldn't every daughter believe she is her father's best girl, and that she holds a special place in her daddy's heart?

That is how God feels towards us. First John 3:1 says, "How great is the love the Father has lavished on us" (NIV). Indeed, His generous, excessive, extravagant luxuries are constantly being poured out on you and me, as the hymnwriter says, "...in fathomless billows of love."

On March 4, 1987, my father graduated to glory. But we never "lost" him—we know exactly where he is. He has left an eternal mark on his family, his friends, his world and especially this daughter.

Each year on March 4, his voice still speaks to our entire family—*to march forth*, to press on. Dad still cheers us on, reminding us never, ever to give up.

God our heavenly Father is cheering you right now, calling you, drawing you, desiring sweet fellowship with you. He longs to spend time alone with you, His daughter, revealing to you the secret treasures of His heart. He invites you to crawl up into His lap, lean your head on His breast, swing your feet back and forth in careless abandon and simply enjoy His presence.

Chapter 39

SOUP FOR LUNCH

Small, random choices sometimes provide a vital turning point in one's life. For me, that happened on a cold November day in Michigan when I stopped at our college snack bar for a cup of hot soup. Served in a styrofoam cup with a plastic spoon, the lunch was ordinary, but it felt hot and tasty to a hurried, hungry young woman on a chilly day.

I had just begun to enjoy my simple lunch when a friend pulled up a chair and sat down. We were soon engaged in an animated conversation. My soup was forgotten for a time, but when my friend rushed off I picked up the white foam cup and resumed eating. Only...

By my college days, I considered myself a singer. I always knew I was destined to sing, but I decided I'd get my college degree in case, just in case, things didn't work out. Then I could fall back on teaching, my second love.

Singing was it, though. While still in high school I had launched my "career," accepting singing dates in nearby bars and clubs. Those weekend experiences in noisy, smoky rooms didn't lead anywhere, but I told myself this was a start. It seemed the logical place to begin.

When not much happened and nobody "discovered" me, I sometimes felt frustrated. But I had a plan. After finishing junior college at home, I would attend the University of Michigan where I could be closer to Motown. That was the center of the musical universe, as far as I was concerned.

Treasure

You can't run with the devil and walk with God.

The Motown sound represented my dream of something new, exciting and modern. Though I had been reared amidst church music, robust singing to the glory of God and by a mother who always sang around the house, and though I served as music director for my father's church, it never occurred to me that the old-time gospel music that surrounded me all my life was *my* music. The gospel music I had known was my parents' and grandparents' music, I thought. It did not fit my cool image, with my miniskirts and high, shiny boots. Church music was too old-fashioned and stale—way too old for me!

Remember, today's contemporary Christian music was extremely young. Early on I did not find much with which I could identify. That's why I saw myself, with my passion for singing, as needing to turn away from gospel and move toward Motown. But those were my ideas, not God's. As it turned out, I never attended the University of Michigan or moved closer to Motown. Instead, there was a scholarship for me at a small Christian college. When I accepted and enrolled there, I entered a new world of serious purpose and commitment.

By now, singing in clubs on Saturday nights and in my father's church on Sundays had made me increasingly more troubled. My heart had become divided. I no longer fully enjoyed either opportunity, sacred or secular. Yet, troubled as I was, I still stubbornly pursued my musical dream.

By contrast, my fellow students held strong Christian attitudes, which had begun to challenge my faith. I saw young people doing things for the Lord, pursuing their dreams with the Lord's plan for their life foremost in their minds. Restless and uncertain, I had begun to search my heart.

My soup had cooled. Tiny pools of grease had formed on top, and a greasy orange ring rimmed the cup. I tried to resume eating, but I couldn't stomach it.

A Bible verse rose to the surface of my mind. The words my father had preached and lived before me all my life truly took root, and the Lord often brought to my mental computer screen something that He wanted me to remember. That day, holding the cup of half-eaten soup, words from Revelation 3:14–16 scrolled

STUFF

Why settle for hamburger when you can have steak?

across my mind's screen. They might as well have started, "Dear Babbie..."

"And to the angel of the church of the Laodiceans write," I read, "... I know your works, that you are neither cold nor hot. I could wish you were cold or hot. So then, because you are lukewarm, and neither cold nor hot, I will vomit you out of My mouth."

God got my attention. His visual aid—that cup of cooling soup—depicted my lifestyle at the time, and I knew it. That day I surrendered my life to God. I had no idea where He would take me or whether I would have to surrender my dream, but I realized with finality that I had too much of the church in me for the world, and too much of the world in me for the church.

That cup of soup represents the revelation that became the catalyst for my present ministry. Soon after that encounter at the snack bar, I took it upon myself to research the church at Laodicea. Here's what I found. The church was financially comfortable. The city was famous for banking and noted for its medical center, which promoted healing for eyes. The area was renowned for its fine fabrics and tapestries. This prosperous community seemed to offer all any citizen would ask. Perhaps that's why the church had become complacent and its fire began to burn low.

The one problem Laodicea had, an inadequate water supply, was overcome by then-modern technology. Someone designed an aqueduct, which could bring water from nearby hot springs into the city. By the time water reached them via their man-made system of pipes, however, it arrived luke-warm. The Lord scarcely had to remind those people how terrible lukewarm water tastes—disgusting enough to make you spit it out.

Lukewarm water tastes terrible. My lukewarm soup made a revolting lunch. I reflected on the truth that it never prospers us to settle for anything less than God's highest and best. As Mom always says, "Why settle for hamburger when you can have steak?"

We believers should not resort to our own half-baked methods and plans. Instead, we should ardently seek God's absolute best. The pure, cool water of His Word continually refreshes those who burn with the zeal of His presence and His calling.

We must refuse to become lukewarm.

Chapter 40

WHO? ME, LORD?

Growing up in our little Michigan church, we were used to taking two offerings—one for the budget, the second for missions. The missions offering was a token. People gave their loose change or maybe a dollar bill. We didn't think about foreign missions much, and we never had a missionary visit our congregation. So we used the offering for local missions: an elderly person who needed a Christmas turkey, or someone who needed a light bill paid.

To my mind, missionaries were always White, attired in black clothing and, if female, always wore their hair in a bun. I never heard of a Black missionary until, in my thirties, I was invited to sing at a missions conference.

This was a conference for African Americans, meant to stir up compassion for those living in Third World countries. I saw Black missionaries and heard their stories. I heard great preaching and teaching. A light turned on in my head, and God spoke to my heart.

In 1990, Charles and I traveled to Africa. There I saw people who looked like me, but spoke another language. For the first time, I felt like a homeless child. I lived in America, but realized afresh that my people had been brought there by force. But Africa, where my ancestors originated, was not my home either. I felt displaced.

I felt also that God was at work in me—He allowed our trip to work out for my people's good, as well as for the good of Charles and me. We both fell in love with the African people. Each year we return to a different country on that huge continent, and each time we find our hearts are challenged and changed through the people's love for the Lord.

We discovered that African brothers and sisters whom we visited, living in Uganda, Ruwanda, Nigeria and South Africa, have a passion for the Lord regardless of their living conditions or their rugged poverty. The Lord is their daily Bread.

I learned also that there are no conditions to the Great Commission. We are *all* commanded to go to the uttermost parts of the earth to tell the good news. Regardless of race, color, age or occupation, we are called to minister. And if we have had a life-changing experience with Christ, we are compelled to go.

After all, if you love someone, you can't wait to tell the world you are in love!

It's the same when it comes to our love for the Lord Jesus Christ, I discovered. I might not fit my own mental stereotype of a missionary, but that does not matter to God. He takes what we offer Him, and He uses it.

Then there's Charles. He didn't fit my stereotypical image of a missionary, either. But I soon saw how perfectly suited he is to minister to the needs of Third World peoples, how his rural background and his practical mind-sets and strengths—not to mention his compassionate heart—minister beyond anything I could imagine.

Charles returns to Uganda and Ruwanda missions two or three times each year. He and others stay with the people, teach lay Christians the principles of God's Word and train them to teach others. The men train the indigenous people how to care for their land, how to improve their water supply and living conditions and how to cook their food safely. It is simple lifestyle evangelism combined with teaching God's Word.

Treasure

God has called you with an eternal purpose. Where you are right now is not where you are going. He still has an appointed task for you to finish.
—Bishop T. D. Jakes

After traveling to Africa a time or two, now it almost feels like home. We are learning some of their language, and they are learning a little of ours. The people are warm-hearted and loving, and God has given us a friendship and kinship with them. Despite our lifestyle differences, we have so much in common.

The word *missionary* might have a foreign sound to you, as it once did to me. I could not have imagined myself in the role.

But don't be put off by the word itself, and don't develop the kind of impressions and prejudice I once held. Think of yourself as a "friend of God" or "one who loves the gospel," and if God provides the opportunity to go to those who need you, be ready to go.

Who, me? Blessed are those who say "Yes, Lord," and go

where He sends them. That, after all, is something any of us can do.

"Yes, Lord." Those two powerful words describe the missionary's heart.

STUFF

*Real-life stuff—
Motel mattresses
are better on the side
away from the phone.*

Chapter 41

OUT OF THE FIRE

Belva Kirk's story begins in 1995. She lived in Magnolia, a little town just outside Houston, Texas, and at that time Belva, her husband, Tommy, and their daughter, Erin, thought their circumstances were difficult. Both parents worked, after all, and carried a lot of responsibility. Belva calls herself a fix-it type, and those days she and Tommy were helping older family members. Their finances were strained.

"But we owned our home," Belva told me. "Money was so tight that we couldn't insure it, but I told myself it was under God's protection. He knew that my house was my security—the only financial security we had.

"On October 30, 1995," Belva continued, "I received a call at work. 'Come home,' they said. 'Your house is on fire.' I was thirty-eight miles away. By the time I got there, the house was nearly destroyed. However, precious pictures and 'memory things' were there."

At age forty-eight, Belva's worst fears had materialized. Her security blanket was gone. They were homeless. "We couldn't turn to our family," she says, "because we were taking care of them."

The Kirks had a wonderful church family, however. "They were tremendous," she said. "A friend immediately took us in, and we three stayed with her for four months. God gave her special grace to allow us to disrupt her life that way."

The fire had devoured Belva's house and virtually all the family's possessions on a Wednesday. On Friday, she was scheduled to attend a church-sponsored ladies' retreat in Houston. "It was already paid for, and everybody insisted that I go," Belva told me. "So I went, thinking, *The chances of my touching God are not all that great. I'm not in a good mood at all.* I had almost no expectations that anything good would come out of that weekend."

But God came to the retreat ahead of Belva, and indeed had a word for her. As she told me five years later, I was the one appointed to deliver that word. "That night, Babbie stepped out and began to sing 'God Has Another Plan,'" she said. "My heart almost stopped."

Belva turned to her friend. "Did you call and tell her to sing that song?"

"No, but Somebody did," her friend whispered.

That special song, written with my friend Cheryl Rogers, came to me soon after my beloved father passed away. It ministered to me then, but I had no idea that years later it would also minister so specifically to a lady whose house had gone up in smoke just hours earlier. Listen to those words:

> Out of the fire
> To the flames of another trial
> Do you feel like your heart
> Has had all it can take
> And nothing is there left to break

In the heat of the fire He will pull you through
When you don't understand He is tried and true
No matter the question
There is an answer for you.

So when the rain falls hard and the storm winds come
And you think it will never blow over
Trouble under your feet, nothing over your head
And you find yourself running for cover
Oh, God has another plan
Remember, God has another plan.

You may be starting all over
And praying that things will get better
You've said all you can say
You've done all that you can
But you're back where you started again
You will find in confusion there is peace at last
You will know that your trials only came to pass
No matter the problem
God's ways are better than best.[1]

"Every word spoke to me," Belva said. "I knew then that God knew me by name and knew my needs. And *I relaxed*. From that point on, it was as if I was being carried."

The peace that passes all understanding that fell on Belva that night never left her. Still, she could not have imagined that it would have to carry her for the next four years.

"The next weekend, my husband and I went to the mall," Belva continued. "He needed clothes. As we approached the store, I could see depression come over him. In the store, it only got worse. He was looking for 'his' clothes, and they were not there. He realized that they were gone, so we left empty-handed.

"'Let's have supper before we leave,' I suggested. As we walked toward the restaurant, I silently prayed, 'Lord, this man needs a touch. He needs help right now.'"

That SOS prayer got an immediate answer. In the restaurant, Tommy Kirk seemed to brighten. He suggested that they return, if there was time, and take another look at a jacket he had seen. They finished their meal just thirty minutes before the mall closed, but hurried back to the clothing store. "When we left, Tommy had a complete new outfit, down to socks. It was as if God had it there waiting for him," Belva said.

After four months of living with their hospitable friend, God told Belva it was time to move on. But there was no place to go. Shelter was scarce in their small community. "I'm the fix-it person in our family," Belva reminded me, "but I couldn't fix this one. I was paralyzed."

A fellow church member told them about a tiny cabin in the woods the family could rent, and they stayed there several months before it was sold. Then they were homeless again.

"Miraculously, someone offered us their garage apartment, one large room and an adjoining bath," Belva told me. "We were thankful to have it. Though we had no privacy, the three of us felt grateful. We lived there until someone offered us a mobile home to rent.

"Does it have walls? And rooms?" Belva asked. "We'll take it!" For four years the family had lived in cramped and often inconvenient places, yet God kept them intact, and Belva still felt His peace. Money continued to be tight, however, and the Kirks could see no way to change their circumstances for the better. Tommy went to school to learn a new trade that he hoped might eventually make them more secure.

Treasure

Do *what you can, for whom you can, with what you have, right where you are.*

"In April of 1998 a gentleman came to our office," Belva continued. "He was a newcomer to town, so I tried to make him welcome and invited him to visit our church. I could see he was a Christian. At some point I told him about our fire. He handed me his business card.

"'You and your husband find the house you want, and I'll help you arrange the financing,' he said. He was a mortgage broker. I was crying when he left our office. I told my friend there, 'I think God just sent me an angel.'"

Tommy and Belva Kirk had not looked for a house to buy. They saw no way they could possibly afford one. They had no money with which to start over, as Tommy was in school at the time. They had never discussed buying a home.

But when Tommy completed his course several months later, he surprised Belva by asking whether she had thought any more about houses. She knew God must have put that thought in her husband's head. And when she telephoned the mortgage broker, he still remembered her and their earlier conversation.

The Kirks found house plans and began the mortgage process, but found themselves $3,800 short of the amount needed to begin building. Discouragement hit them both hard. "I fussed at God a little that night," Belva confessed, "and He whispered in my ear, 'Belva, if the mortgage company builds it, you won't know I did it.'"

She took her hands off the problem. One night soon after, while reading her Bible, she was amazed to find a story that paralleled her own. Chapter 1 in the Book of Haggai tells how the children of Israel had returned home from exile and were grumbling about all their lack. The Lord told them to look around. "You're so busy worrying about your things," He told them, "that you are not concerned that My house is in ruins." He instructed them to rebuild His house so He could take pleasure in it and receive glory there.

The message electrified Belva. "It moved me deeply to realize that God and I had the same heart's desire for a house we could live in and take pleasure in, one that He could receive glory in.

"When we finally could start building, I had that passage, Haggai 1:7–8, inscribed on the foundation of our porch so people would know it was built so we could take pleasure in and glorify God. We 'took possession of the land' in August of 1999.

"It took four years of waiting for God—homeless. But by

STUFF

By perseverance the snail reached the ark.
—Charles Spurgeon

this time I had come to see that God had moved into the house in my heart. In this one area of my life, if no other, I was able to give it all to Him. This was one time in my life when I didn't try to fix it. This one time, I stepped back and let God build the house."

Mortgage arrangements took longer than usual, yet Belva didn't fret or try to speed things up. Nor did she hover over the builders as they worked. At last she truly surrendered her housing and security needs into the hands of God.

You might call the new house a miracle. In her heart, Belva knows that the real miracle took place when she purposed, over those four years, to trust God to the utmost with her deepest needs. "The house God wanted to build for me is a place for Him to dwell in my heart," she explained. "I pray that my heart may be such a comfortable place for Him to live that He never wants to leave."

She admits that occasionally the devil throws a dart at her, and she flinches for a moment at the thought of taking on a thirty-year mortgage during their fifties. Or she's reminded, when she writes the mortgage check, that this large monthly sum is something they once did not have to pay.

"Things have not been smooth," Belva reflects, "but the changes were easy enough. When the fire comes, or any other unexpected disaster, I've learned that before you rebuild, it's wise to first build a place where God can live in your heart.

"Then move forward. Don't rely on your feelings. I have learned my feelings are not reliable. But He is, and He will rebuild your heart and your circumstances and your life. As Babbie's song says, God has a plan for you."

[1] "God Has Another Plan" by Babbie Mason and Cheryl Rogers. Copyright © 1992 by Word Music, Inc. All rights reserved. Used by permission. International rights secured.

Chapter 42

SHE AIN'T HEAVY— SHE'S MY SISTER

You meet some powerful people in the Christian music world, individuals with tremendous talents and awesome personal testimonies. Singer Delia Roman, one of those shining stars, is a beautiful young woman who has a powerful anointing, a voice as big as Texas and a love of God that touches every note she sings.

Delia became confined to a wheelchair when a 1987 automobile accident left her a paraplegic. Later, she was diagnosed with a brain tumor, which the Lord healed. Such life-changing events might have stopped a lesser woman, but not Delia. "People say I'm confined to a wheelchair," she quips, "But I say the chair is confined to me. After all, I control it!"

Delia gets around. She ministers everywhere. "But it wasn't that way at first," she confessed. "Deeply depressed, I'd ask myself, Why should I get out of bed? Take a shower? Get dressed? I'm not going anywhere."

Wrong! God had other intentions, plus a secret weapon He provided so Delia could regain a fulfilling life. He provided Adrianne, her friend and manager, who never intended that Delia would hide and subside. "When invitations came

I'd say, 'Ask my manager,'" Delia said. "Then Adrianne would tell me, 'You've got to do this,' and she'd make me get out of bed and get dressed, and she'd haul me outside and into her car.

"She carried me piggyback fashion on her back, forcing me to get out for church or Bible study or even just for a hot dog!"

I last saw Delia in Nashville at the Gospel Music Association Week, a huge convention the Christian music industry sponsors each year. We were included in a Christian album project called "Sisters," a collection of songs written, sung by and intended for women—sisters in the Lord. Our group included different races, ages and cultures. Delia, for example, is Hispanic, while I am African American.

Treasure

Thank God for what you have. Trust God for what you need.

So we got together to celebrate our unity and diversity, female musicians of every genre, and we cut our album. Vestal Goodman, Gloria Gaither, Danniebelle Hall, Tremaine Hawkins, CeCe and Vicki Winans and others recorded music to minister powerfully to women. We were to premiere our album by singing one of the selections at the convention.

Now several of us, including Delia and her manager friend, Adrianne, were gathered backstage preparing to walk on. We noticed that a little stairway led to the stage—and there was no wheelchair access. The soloist onstage had reached the climax of his song—a piece titled, "Lord, Use Me."

"If You can use anything, use me," he concluded. Adrianne instantly lifted Delia, slung her across her back and carried her up the steps. The rest of us stood frozen, totally astonished, as Adrianne sang along with the soloist, "If You can use anything, Lord, use me . . . but not as a pack mule, Lord." Delia, meanwhile, was giggling.

The moment astounded us. To break the tension a little, I softly sang, "She ain't heavy, she's my sister," and we all cracked up. And then we entered the stage and sang a perfect musical picture of what had just happened:

> We are sisters, sisters in the Lord,
> Our faith in common, sisters in the Lord
> No matter how the world defines us,
> Nothing can break the tie that binds us
> We are sisters in the Lord.[1]

Backstage, I guess the Lord was telling us, "I can show you, better than you can sing it, what unity and sisterhood are all about." That vivid snapshot stayed in my mind. It showed us so well what it means to bear another's burden, to stand together, to meet one another's needs. For me, it was a poignant moment.

STUFF

If Jesus Christ is in your heart, notify your face.

213

And it made me curious about Adrianne.

"Adrianne has been an amazing sister in the Lord," Delia told me. "She's not much for words, but she's mighty in action. She doesn't boast about her faith, but she always walks it. After my accident she never allowed me to slip into a depression so deep I could not come out. She was there for me, constantly.

"At the concert that night she simply did what had to be done. Others have told me how it moved them. Another brother in the audience shared with me that he saw us in silhouette behind the curtain. I couldn't imagine that, because the lights were not up yet. But he saw us despite the low lights, and it made him weep. Something so simple, yet the Lord spoke so loudly."

That night Delia and Adrianne illustrated unforgettably what Jesus Christ does for all of us. In Matthew 11, He invites us to "come to Me, all you who labor and are heavy laden, and I will give you rest. Take My yoke upon you and learn from Me, for I am gentle and lowly in heart, and you will find rest for your souls. For My yoke is easy and My burden is light" (vv. 28–30).

When He carries us, He carries our burdens to the foot of the cross and lays them there. Therefore, as Delia and Adrianne showed us, we can do the same for our brother or sister.

---

[1] "Sisters" by Dick and Melody Tunney. Copyright © 1994 BMG Songs, Inc. and Dick and Mel Music. (ASCAP). All rights on behalf of Dick and Mel Music administered by BMG Songs, Inc. All rights reserved. Used by permission. BMG Music Publishing controls 100% worldwide.

Chapter 43

OFFICER CHAMPION ARRIVES

Kenn Mann had several things on his mind as he drove home. Well past midnight, he had just finished his keyboard gig at the famous hotel where he worked. The heavy fog rolling in was making the bad section of town through which he had to drive seem even more dangerous. And worse, he had discovered his wallet was missing.

"I sure hope it's at home," Kenn worried.

The empty street seemed eerie and threatening, but there was a green light ahead. Only a couple more miles to go, and he'd be home looking for his wallet. But as Kenn proceeded through the light on that deserted main thoroughfare, car lights suddenly appeared. Kenn realized another car was headed straight toward him.

"*You're going to hit me!*" Kenn turned the wheel hard, trying to give the other driver the road, but the fellow plowed into the rear of Kenn's car with an ear-splitting crash that sent both vehicles spinning.

"I was able to get out of my car," Kenn related, "and was relieved to see the other driver get out of his. He was the biggest Black gentleman I'd ever seen.

"'You ran the red light,' I told him."

Then things got ugly. "You ran the light," the other man barked, with considerable profanity. He walked toward Kenn menacingly and snarled. "I'm going to kill you. I'm going to beat you to death."

"I knew he meant what he was saying," Kenn told me. "I knew he would kill me. There was nobody to stop him. Here's this fat little White guy up against this eight-foot tall Black man…"

Treasure

The champion is not the one who never loses. The champion is the one who never quits.

"I'm going to beat you to death," the man repeated, and came toward Kenn.

"Jesus!" That one word was all Kenn said. Actually, he whispered the name. At that instant, a white van appeared from nowhere. The driver rolled down his window and called out, "Is that Kenn Mann?"

"Yes," Kenn replied, startled. "Who are you?"

"I am Officer Champion. Are you in trouble?"

"Yes, I am. This gentleman ran a red light and hit my car." As Kenn said those words, he suddenly thought, *I am in trouble. I don't have my driver's license!*

"I'm a police officer," the man said, turning to Kenn's adversary. "Sir, is there trouble here?" The big man backed away and said no. By now the officer had phoned for help, and another police car arrived. "I told both officers the truth about the accident," Kenn said, "and explained that I had misplaced my wallet."

"That's OK," Officer Champion told his colleague. "I can vouch for this man's identity." The incident soon was resolved, and Kenn drove home.

Here's the rest of the story. Officer Champion, who drove up through the mist at the split second when Kenn needed him most, was someone Kenn did not know. Kenn had once served as minister of music where the officer had attended church. The officer remembered Kenn, but no matter how hard Kenn racked his brain, he did not remember Officer Champion. He says he wouldn't recognize the man's face if he saw it today.

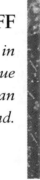

STUFF

Anger is a condition in which the tongue works faster than the mind.

"I wondered if God had sent me an angel," Kenn said. "I have never seen Officer Champion since that night." I asked Kenn if he had ever settled the strange events of that night in his mind.

"Yes. I called on the name of Jesus," he told me. "I said His name in a whisper, but I said it.

"That night I knew I didn't have a chance. Then Officer Champion showed up. God protected me and saved me. After I reached my apartment that night and began thanking God, I realized again how amazingly God had protected me in that deserted and violent area of town."

What would Kenn tell others who might face a similarly dangerous moment?

"When the situation looks hopeless and the tunnel has no light, call on Jesus. He comes through. I just whispered 'Jesus,' and He was there. He came in the form of a person. He also could come through a telephone call, words in your book of devotions or a friend who encourages you."

Remember His name. JESUS. Sometimes that's the only prayer you find yourself able to pray. It is enough. Officer Champion is the undefeated, undiputed and all-powerful Champion of heaven and earth, and He will arrive. When you are in trouble, your Champion will recognize you and vouch for you. Jesus knows your name.

Chapter 44

HE'LL FIND A WAY

The harvested cantaloupes were big, juicy and sweet during the summer of 1982, when I was expecting Chaz, our second son. I craved cantaloupes, ate almost nothing else and had to make regular supermarket runs to restock.

For me, things always seem to happen at the supermarket. It was at the produce counter that I spotted a short, blond-haired woman who was there on the same mission. She looked as if she knew how to choose melons. Southerners know how to heft a melon, sniff it and thump it before they select the perfect one.

"How do they feel?" I asked my fellow shopper.

"We'll each find a couple of good ripe ones," she promised.

And that's how I met my songwriter friend Donna Douglas from Ft. Lauderdale, Florida. We soon discovered we had more than melons in common.

When she looked up from the melon bin, she recognized me, because I had sung at her church only two weeks earlier. She introduced herself as a fellow songwriter and soon was dashing out to her car to bring me samples of her work. Thus began our God-given, very fruitful and wonderful friendship.

Soon Donna Douglas, my husband, Charles, and I would find ourselves attending the same Colorado music conference, and like me, she also would come home with the miserable feeling that she had struck out. Those feelings immediately became insignificant to her, however, when she learned there had been a terrible tragedy in her church family. Their choir president's two-year-old daughter and his mother-in-law had been found drowned in a swimming pool.

On hearing the news Donna immediately prayed, "Lord, please don't let me have to see them at church tomorrow, because I don't know what to say."

Treasure

Joy is not the absence of sorrow, but the presence of God.

The next day as Donna stepped out of her car in the church parking lot, the grieving couple pulled up alongside her vehicle. In her efforts to comfort them, Donna said, "If God can paint sunsets, plant the stars in space and conquer death, He can find a way to help you get through this."

That heartbreaking episode led her to write "He'll Find a Way," a song I have sung hundreds of times in public. But there was one unforgettable time when it ministered especially powerfully to my entire family—including me.

In the fall of 1986, I received an invitation to sing at a Billy Graham Crusade. Prayerfully, I chose two of the most meaningful songs I know, "Yes, My God Is Real" and Donna's song, "He'll Find A Way," to sing at the crusade.

Months later, on March 4, 1987, I received the stunning news that my daddy had passed away suddenly, following a heart attack. The blow was enormous. Not only had I lost my father, but also my pastor during all my growing-up years as well. The day of his funeral seemed the darkest in our close-knit family's experience. At the church, where I took my usual seat behind the piano, I remembered how I'd always joked that no matter how packed out the church might be, I always had a good seat up front. I felt if there ever was a day when I needed to be at my familiar duty post, where I felt most at home, that was the day I should be behind that piano. I played and sang at my daddy's service, and God comforted me.

By Monday, my sister and three brothers and I had to start thinking about returning to our respective homes. But that evening the Billy Graham Crusade "happened" to air, and we all gathered to watch. With spouses and children and our newly widowed mother, my siblings and I made a tight circle around the television set to bond once again as a family.

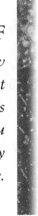

STUFF

No matter how old you are—or what your relationship is with your parents—you miss them terribly after they die.

We felt solemn and quiet. Then, as we watched, there was Babbie Mason singing "My God Is Real." Listening, the air around us seemed to fill with our silent "amens." After that, as if I were hearing it for the very first time, I heard myself sing Donna's song, "He'll Find a Way."

> If He can paint a sunset
> And put the stars in place,
> If He can raise up mountains
> And calm the storm-tossed waves,
> If He can conquer death forever
> And open heaven's gate,
> Then I know for you
> He'll find a way.[1]

My heart began to fill with peace. What a God we serve! How amazing that He would allow Babbie Mason not only to minister to her family at the saddest time of their lives, but even to minister also to herself! From my own mouth had come the words that touched and reassured me, the very words I needed most.

For my mother, my siblings and myself—and for all those who weep and mourn—yes, "My God Is Real."

And, "He'll Find a Way."

---

[1] "He'll Find a Way" by Donna Douglas. Copyright © 1987 by C.A. Music (a div. of C.A. Records, Inc.). All rights reserved. Used by permission.

Chapter 45

RIDING THE STORM

My mother says storms are like life—you are either in one, coming out of one or heading into one. Nature's storms can't be averted, but the whole world desperately prepared itself against an expected cataclysm named "the Y2K bug" and its potential for wreaking havoc. For months on end we worried obsessively about computers, businesses, government, traffic, banks—you name it.

Prior to New Year's Eve 1999, many stocked up on food, filled gasoline tanks in cars and bought flashlights, generators, firewood and water. As it turned out, we prepared exceptionally well for a disaster that never arrived.

The one that did arrive that month, however, brought thousands of us to our knees. Y2K had come and gone with a yawn, but three weeks later Mother Nature's winter storms brought much of the eastern and midwestern United States to a standstill. One storm after another dumped vicious loads of snow, sleet, freezing rain, fog, hail and every other possible variation of winter weather on us. "The big storm," as they called it, disrupted virtually everything. It closed schools, caused thousands of traffic accidents, disrupted airport services and brought businesses to a halt.

Amidst all this, Charles and I were scheduled to fly to Cincinnati. What to do, Lord? The sky outside our Atlanta windows shone bright and sunny, but the weatherman assured us that the storm was on its way. We thought it would be a good idea to check with the airline. Sure enough, our flight had been canceled. When they were able to book us on another flight, however, we figured the Lord must be telling us to go. God willing, we could return the next day as scheduled.

Treasure

Anxiety is the interest paid on trouble before it is due.
—Dean William R. Inge

Soon after we departed Atlanta the storm blew in, crippling the city. By now we found ourselves a thousand miles from home in Cincinnati, with visions of being snowed in for days. Freezing rain was pelting Atlanta, snapping tree limbs, downing power lines and closing main arteries into the city. Hundreds of travelers headed into Atlanta for the Super Bowl game became stranded along the roadsides.

Meanwhile, a major new snowstorm was about to roll into Cincinnati. We prayed that God would help us get out before it arrived and help us return to Atlanta safely despite our town's unusually terrible weather.

After several delays at the airport, at last they de-iced our plane, and we departed Cincinnati. By that time our window of opportunity had become critically short. We took off in the face of the approaching storm, anxiously flying into skies that definitely did not look friendly.

As I looked into the inky clouds above Cincinnati and felt the alarmingly bumpy turbulence, my body tensed. But once we climbed above the storm system and broke through the threatening clouds, suddenly we were soaring through a limitless, serene, clear blue sky! As we watched, amazed and entranced by the beauty, we saw a gorgeous orange-streaked horizon where the sun was beginning to set. Only God could have fingerpainted that enormous sky. I realized with awe that He was flying with us. He was beneath us, above us, beside us.

Even so, we knew potential danger lurked ahead. Surely the freezing rains had turned Atlanta's hilly streets into sheer glass, and the tall pine trees, heavy with ice, would have snapped and taken power lines with them. I dreaded our aircraft's descent. "But the pilots know what they are doing," I comforted myself. "They have radar to guide us down safely."

STUFF

Thunder is good, thunder is impressive, but it is the lightning that does the work.
—Mark Twain

We need not have worried. When our aircraft broke through the clouds above Atlanta we saw no sleet, snow or freezing rain. We drove home without incident.

God goes with us through every storm. He gives us faith, which, like radar, can guide us through places where our visibility is limited. And our faith radar always can take us just one more step, though we cannot see what's immediately ahead.

God's Holy Spirit occupies the control tower, and He guides us perfectly. When He leads us so gently and safely, we need never fear life's turbulence or its stormy takeoffs and landings.

If you are riding through a storm, coming out of a storm or headed for a fearsome storm, remember that God goes with you. We can prepare for even the worst by hiding God's Word in our hearts that we may not sin against Him. We can face the most troublesome or terrifying events of our life, knowing that His Word will strengthen us and make us able to stand.

He who will never leave us or forsake us knows about our every heartbeat. He lives within us, and He dwells above us, beneath us and beside us, all the days—even the stormiest days—of our life.

Chapter 46

A WAKE-UP CALL

My brother Ben felt great anticipation about his upcoming trip to Georgianna, Alabama, where he would preside at our cousin's wedding. You've never heard of Georgianna? That's funny. Neither had the travel agent apparently, or the airline, or the automobile rental company...

"I'll never forget my first visit," Ben said. "It had so much meaning for me. Our entire clan gathered in a tiny settlement that normally must be population 10. I saw the 400 prime acres where our family grew cotton and tall pine trees, and I heard our great-uncle's stories about boyhood pranks with his White playmate and close friends."

Ben's account of that first trip to Georgianna makes it seem almost dreamlike. He recalls with great delight some of the family scenes, the wonderful stories and meeting kinfolk he had never met before, all in that rich, deeply rural corner of the South. But perhaps the most meaningful aspect of the entire trip, for Ben, was his preaching the Sunday sermon at the old church our great-grandfather founded and pastored.

But if Ben's first trip to Georgianna seemed dreamlike, the

second trip—or at least his travel experience—became anything but dreamy.

"My wife made the airline reservations through a travel agent and reserved a rental car," Ben said. "Relatives said there was a forty-five minute drive from the airport to Georgianna, and several had volunteered to meet me at the airport. But I wanted a car so I could explore our old homeplace. I had arranged a four-day weekend so I could counsel the bride- and groom-to-be prior to their wedding, and so I could enjoy a second family reunion."

Treasure

Patience is the ability to idle your motor when you feel like stripping your gears.

But Ben arrived at the wrong airport, one that was three hours away from Greenville, where he should have landed. The rental car was there, however, so he drove on in to Greenville, hoping someone there could help him find his way to a place nobody had ever heard of.

"I made it, and the four-day visit blessed me," Ben said. "The wedding was a fairly elaborate affair at the small country church, with the reception held at a rented hall 'in town.' My visit was drawing to a close. Now I had to figure out how to make my return flight by eight o'clock in the morning!"

Ben figured that if he left no later than 4 A.M., he'd have time for the three-hour drive and the time needed to return his rented car—if he winked at the speed limits. But after returning to his cousins' house late that evening, the family entered into wonderful conversation and time slipped away. It was well past midnight when Ben retired to the little room they had prepared for him. He set the clock radio for 3:30 A.M., thinking that a couple of hours of sleep might do him good.

Hardly had he dropped off to sleep, however, when he was awakened by a loud buzz. "Not the alarm clock," Ben said, "but a mosquito. An Alabama-August-dive-bombing-bloodsucking mosquito! I listened, and the noise stopped. I swatted my forehead. A moment's silence, and the humming began again. I had missed him! Now the humming seemed far away, somewhere in the distance, out of reach in the quiet, quiet, darkness.

"Then, I heard it again! The kamikaze drone dove for my ear—so again I swatted and missed. After the third attack I sat up in bed, reached for the pull-string for the overhead light, and squinted at the clock. THREE FORTY-FIVE! The alarm had failed to sound.

STUFF

Have you ever noticed that when you wave to people in the country, they always wave back?

"I dressed quickly and slipped out of the house without rousing anyone—and made the dash to the airport. I turned in the rental car and made it to the departure gate with only minutes to spare.

"Thank You, Lord, for your involvement in even the last-minute details of my life. Yes, Lord, thank You for sending that Alabama-August-dive-bombing-bloodsucking mosquito.

"That mosquito knew where to find me in Georgianna, Alabama, a town nobody in the travel industry could seem to find!"

Whether we travel to the North Pole or deep into the Alabama piney woods, God knows exactly where we are. The Bible tells us He is interested in even the tiniest details of our lives. We are never out of God's reach or outside His care. And as Ben learned, He can always find a messenger to send to us—even a tiny, loud mosquito.

Chapter 47

～

ONE DAY AT A TIME

Sometimes life brings us to a sudden, unexpected halt, then forces us to learn how to live again, one painful day at a time. For Benita Dear, my younger sister, the unthinkable happened in 1997, when she lost her husband, Tyrone, to cancer.

The story of widowhood always differs from woman to woman, but in one way at least, it's the same for all. "My story is still in progress," Benita says. And that, for a woman experiencing widowhood, is almost universally true.

Benita and Tyrone's story is a happy one, filled with the goodness of God. Young, energetic and bright, each brought a lot to their marriage. As upwardly mobile professionals, they earned promotions and prosperity. As a couple in love, they enjoyed life to the hilt. And as proud parents of three live-wire children, they felt they had it all.

"We enjoyed our life," Benita said. "We had three precious children, and we were prospering. The world was our oyster. I often thanked the Lord that He gave me such a wonderful man. Tyrone was a great father. He was respected in our community, a church-going man, a person with such a good mind. He wasn't perfect, I guess, but he was my friend, my confidant and my lover."

After building excellent careers in corporate America, Tyrone and Benita decided to bring their combined expertise to a business venture of their own. "I left my job first, and in 1994 we started our business, which immediately took off," Benita said. "Tyrone resigned his position in 1997 to join me. This business was our mutual decision, and its immediate success gave us such joy and satisfaction."

Treasure

To get out of a difficulty, one must usually go through it.

Benita noted that the business start-up blossomed overnight, seemingly with little effort on their parts. The couple was putting their stamp on their very own enterprise, and could not have been happier. They were a blessed family.

"People would ask how we could work together all day and get along so well," Benita reminisced. "That was never a problem for us. Oh, a couple of times we got testy and I quit. But Tyrone would say, 'Then I won't pay you.' We'd come to our senses, laugh, he'd 'rehire' me, and I'd get my paycheck. But we enjoyed our work, our play and our worship together."

In early 1995, Benita says, Tyrone decided he needed to lose a few pounds, and put himself on a diet. "The weight came off, and we thought that was wonderful," she recalled. "Then he began getting tired. Close to Christmas, he saw his doctor, who was not alarmed, but the week before Christmas, Tyrone fainted. I insisted on driving him to the hospital."

Then their roller-coaster ride began. Tests revealed a stomach tumor and doctors recommended immediate surgery. But Tyrone, a praying man, said he needed to go before the Lord and seek His advice about what to do. The surgery took place the following February, and seemed successful.

"We were ecstatic," Benita told me. "The word *cancer* sets off an alarm like no other. But we prayed and stayed optimistic. We were so thankful for that good outcome."

The cancer returned. By the spring of 1997, Tyrone again began feeling tired. But the couple thought that was understandable, since he was working so hard at their business, which was booming. He worked long hours, traveling, networking and doing everything else a CEO does. The couple did not connect Tyrone's fatigue to cancer.

Not only did he have cancer again, but this time it was inoperable. It had spread too far; there was nothing doctors could do.

"Still, we believed the Lord would give us a breakthrough," Benita told me. "Even as his health swiftly declined, even when he became bedridden, Tyrone and I kept the faith. I never thought we would lose him. Tyrone fought a good fight, but the Lord allowed him to graduate to heaven."

Nothing prepares a devoted wife for the loss of her husband. "I had tried always to be such a 'together' woman," my sister told me honestly. "I took pride in doing things well, seeing that our kids were well fed, clothed and parented. Keeping our house just so, and staying professional in my work life. These things mattered to me.

"Now, I had a million questions for God. Why had this happened? How could I manage? And did God actually think I could handle everything alone? Rev. Jeremiah Wright, Jr., pastor of Trinity United Church of Christ in Chicago, warned me, 'Benita, you will experience some anger at the Lord.'

"I told him, 'How could I? I am in such dire need, I cannot fathom the idea of being angry with God.' But that anger did erupt. I'd think, *You could have healed Tyrone, but You didn't. Do You think I can raise these children by myself? Or that my children don't need a father? What do I do about the loneliness? How do I handle the pain?*"

Bottom line, however, Benita trusted God. Sore and bruised as her heart might feel, she did not allow the anger that sometimes surfaced to overshadow the love she felt toward Him. "I will not shut Him out," she declares.

And that, no doubt, is why Benita, and so many other women like her, find it possible to take their unwelcome widowhood step by step, one day at a time. And why, as the years pass, Benita calls it an evolving story, one with many surprises.

"I'm no longer a 'together' woman," she told me. "I'm realizing that God holds me together and holds my world together. Sometimes I have to rely on other people, a new thing for me. Some days the beds don't get made, and though the house is still standing, it looks a mess!"

Benita's kids are growing, and their many activities keep her busy. Between their needs, her home and the business, she says that everyday life can become a major undertaking. This once super-efficient woman says, "I have the support of God, my family and some people in my life that I never dreamed would enter it. Some have been so motivational to me, especially on those days when I didn't even want to face life.

"God sent the people I needed to help me. Without that, I might have thrown in the towel a long time ago. I am still grieving, but have taken one major step—I have accepted Tyrone's death. I no longer tell the Lord, 'I can't do this.'"

A little more than two years after the shock of losing her husband, Benita Dear has a far broader perspective on God's part in preparing her for the event. "He led Tyrone and me to start our own business. If I were in corporate America today, working an eight-to-five job, there's no way I could adequately parent my kids.

"Our business allows me to be flexible. I can see to breakfast, homework and other family matters and fit my work life in around the needs of my children. Tyrone took his family responsibilities very seriously. He made sure he took care of his family very well. I see the hand of God in so many of our practical deci-

STUFF

Give God what's right, not what's left.

sions, which mean so much to me now, as a woman who has become head of her household.

"Two years after Tyrone's death, my faith reassures me, day by day. My faith tells me God is in control. Even at those times when I felt too overwhelmed to pray, I knew God was there, I also learned that many, many other people, more than you dream, are praying for you when you cannot pray for yourself."

One step at a time, one day at a time, Benita believes God walks with the woman who feels she is alone. One prayer at a time, one friend at a time, she becomes stronger and more confident of His presence and comfort.

Benita Dear, who says her story is a story in progress, also knows it is a love story of the highest order. It's a story of grief, helplessness and even anger, but even more, it's a story of surrender, new growth and ultimate peace.

Like every other story God writes, Benita feels certain that hers too will have a triumphant outcome.

Chapter 48

PRICELESS TREASURE

Did you know that diamonds, the world's most favored jewels, were first found in the sand and gravel from the beds of streams? Did you know that later on, diamonds were found deep in the earth in rock formations? I found this to be an interesting fact about diamonds. Did you know that it requires sometimes as much as twenty tons of gravel to yield one diamond? One more question: Did you know that before a diamond reveals its beautiful brilliance it must be taken from deep within the earth, crushed, sorted, cut and polished?

No, this is not a trivia test on diamonds. This is a humble attempt to reveal an extravagant promise. God wants to turn every one of life's toughest situations into a treasure that He can use for your good and His glory. God wants you to know that there is not one single situation that you have ever encountered or will ever encounter that is beyond His control. Furthermore, whatever touches your life must first be filtered through the sovereignty of His big hand. You may feel as if you have been pulled, crushed, sorted and cut. Whatever that earthly circumstance is, somewhere, some way, somehow it is achieving for you a priceless, heavenly treasure.

This final chapter serves as one last reminder, one final word of comfort, that while you may be walking through a fiery situation, God—just as He was with the three Hebrew children—is right there in the furnace with you. While you may be right in the middle of a wicked storm, God—just as He was with His disciples on the Sea of Galilee—is riding it out with you. While you may feel that you have been swallowed up and trapped by some force that is bigger and stronger than you, God—just as He was with Jonah—is right there in the smelly, tangled-up seaweed of your predicament. He is not *on* the way. He is *there*, right now. As He promised in Matthew 28:20, "And surely I am with you always, to the very end of the age" (NIV).

Treasure

Whatever that earthly circumstance is, somewhere, some way, somehow it is achieving for you a priceless, heavenly treasure.

One more thing I want you to remember: You are precious to God. You may not feel like it, but you are. You may have a few bumps and bruises from being tossed around on the playing field of life, but you still are invaluable. You may be down, but you are not out. You may have had some dirt on you from past scuffles, but God welcomes you with open arms and is able to give you a clean start.

I heard this awesome illustration recently that I must share with you. Let's say I had the wonderful privilege of showing up on your doorstep and spending some time with you.

Then at the end of our meeting, I wanted to bless you by giving you a nice, clean, crisp one hundred dollar bill. Would you take it? *For sake of the illustration, please say yes.* What if I crumpled up the one hundred dollar bill in my hand? Would you still take it? *Work with me here; I'm going somewhere with this, so say yes. Thank you.* What if I crumpled it up, threw it down on the ground, and while I was stomping on it, it got covered with mud? Would you still take it? *You're an old pro at this now. Thanks for saying yes.* And why would you take it? Because you realize that even though the bill is wrinkled, stomped on and has mud on it, it has not lost one cent of its value.

That same wonderful certainty holds true for you. Regardless of your situation, the outcome remains the same. You matter to God, and He loves you. You are priceless and precious to Him. Remember, nothing, absolutely nothing, can ever change that.

Being the teacher that I am, I'd like to leave you with

STUFF

The mediocre teaching tells. The good teacher explains. The superior teacher demonstrates. The great teacher inspires.
—Dr. William Arthur Ward

a homework assignment. Ask God to give you the spiritual wherewithal to recognize the potential to find the "treasure in earthen vessels," as Paul calls it in 2 Corinthians 4:7. Ask God to help you to focus, not on the decaying container, your frail and fragile humanity, but on the rare and priceless treasure—the power of God—that is contained inside. This assignment is not for the cowardly. It takes guts to choose the right tools and to go and dig up hard and fallow ground. It takes courage to go treasure hunting. No doubt, you'll ache because of it. You may break a sweat for it. But pretty soon, as you turn over the hard clumps of clay, out of your peripheral vision you will spot the shiny gleam of a nugget—a promise from God's heart that He is working for you, in you and through you.

The same words that the apostle Paul used to close the third chapter of the Book of Ephesians, I will use to close this one. "Now to him who is able to do immeasurably more than all we ask or imagine, according to his power that is at work within us, to him be glory in the church and in Christ Jesus throughout all generations, for ever and ever! Amen" (vv. 20–21, NIV).

~

At BABBIE MASON MINISTRIES, we endeavor to be an encouragement through music ministry, songwriting, public speaking, teaching, the television talk show *Babbie's House* and our annual *Babbie Mason Music Seminar*, a conference for singers and songwriters.

For more information concerning Babbie Mason Ministries, please contact:

Babbie Mason Ministries
1480-F Terrell Mill Road, Suite 291
Marietta, Georgia 30067
770-952-1443

You can also visit us online at
www.babbie.com

You can experience more of God's grace & love!

If you would like free information on how you can know God more deeply and experience His grace, love and power more fully in your life, simply write or e-mail us. We'll be delighted to send you information that will be a blessing to you.

To check out other titles from **Creation House** that will impact your life, be sure to visit your local Christian bookstore, or call this toll-free number:

1-800-599-5750

For free information from Creation House:

CREATION HOUSE
600 Rinehart Rd.
Lake Mary, FL 32746
www.creationhouse.com

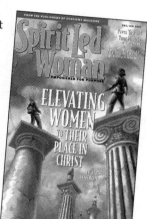